MW01608991

RIVER LORDS

Library and Archives Canada Cataloguing in Publication

Peyton, Amy Louise, 1920-
River lords : father and son / Amy Louise Peyton. -- 2nd ed.

Includes bibliographical references.
ISBN 1-894463-51-X

1. Peyton, John, 1747?-1827. 2. Peyton, John, 1793-1879. 3.
Newfoundland and Labrador--History. 4. Beothuk Indians. 5.
Pioneers--Newfoundland and Labrador--Exploits River Region--Biography. 6.
Exploits River Region (N.L.)--Biography. 7. Newfoundland and
Labrador--Biography. I. Title.

FC2171.1.P4P49 2005   971.8'01'0922   C2005-901980-8

PRINTED IN CANADA

FLANKER PRESS LTD.
ST. JOHN'S, NL, CANADA
TOLL FREE: 1-866-739-4420
WWW.FLANKERPRESS.COM

Cover photo: Brian Bursey

Canada

We acknowledge the financial support of the Government of Canada through the Book
Publishing Industry Development Program (BPIDP) for our publishing program.

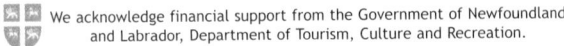

Canada Council   Conseil des Arts
for the Arts   du Canada

We acknowledge the support of the Canada Council for the Arts
which last year invested $20.3 million in writing and publishing throughout Canada.

We acknowledge financial support from the Government of Newfoundland
and Labrador, Department of Tourism, Culture and Recreation.

RIVER LORDS

FATHER AND SON

Amy Louise Peyton

FLANKER PRESS LTD.
ST. JOHN'S, NL
2005

MAP OF NEWFOUNDLAND

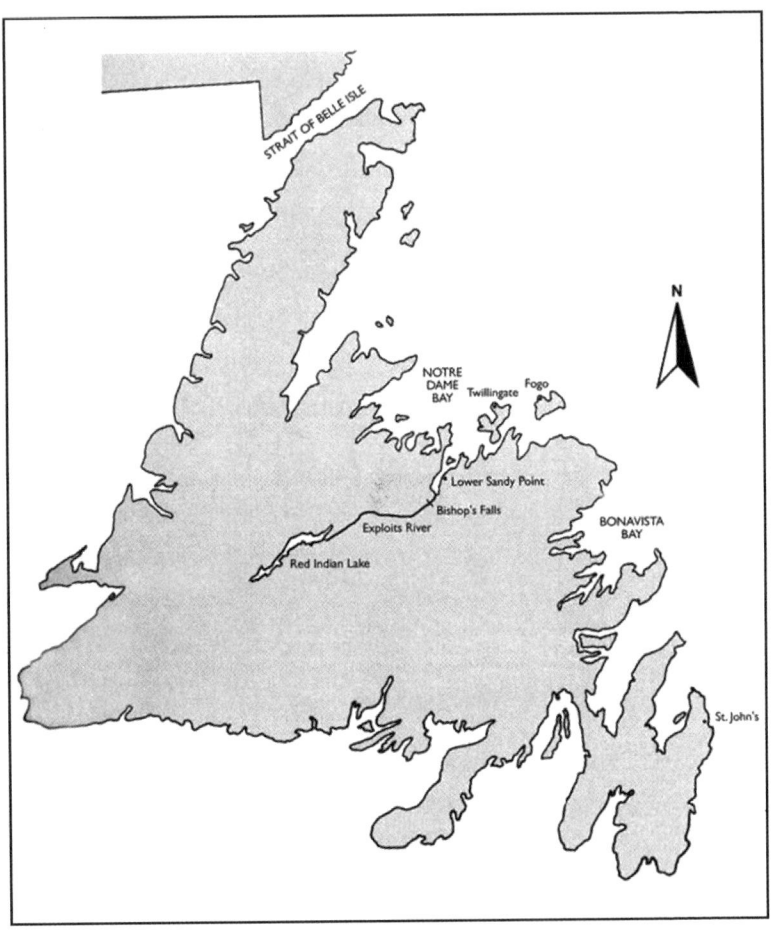

TABLE OF CONTENTS

LIST OF ILLUSTRATIONS

ACKNOWLEDGEMENTS

It is not enough to just acknowledge the help and advice which I received while researching and writing this book.

None of this would have been possible without my husband, Ernest, a paternal great-grandson of John Peyton Jr. He had carefully preserved the papers, books, documents and correspondence of his ancestors, which provided me with much of the information in the book. He bore with me as I worked on and discussed the book. He must often have wished that I had never begun! To Ernest I owe my deepest gratitude for his devotion and support. I am delighted that the book includes some of his poems. The first, on the dedication page, is a measure of the feeling which he has for the subject.

To my daughter Evelyn, I owe profound gratitude for her patience and help in editing the second draft; and to my daughter Carol, heartfelt thanks for her willingness to listen and to advise when I needed her help.

Great appreciation is expressed to Judy Gibson, my editor, for all the help she has given me and for having faith in my work.

Thanks is due in great measure to Edgar Baird of Gander, a maternal great-grandson of John Peyton Jr. His collection of papers, documents and private letters of Peyton ancestors has provided me with information which helped greatly to fill in the "missing links."

Thanks are also due to the Gander librarians, especially to Mrs. Rita Tompkins; to the Provincial Archives of Newfoundland and Labrador; to Mr. V.D. Ponton of Bournemouth, England, for the history of Hengist Masonic Lodge of Christchurch.

My sons Dunley, Kent and Brent helped me with their good wishes and encouragement, and I thank them both.

PREFACE

Since the end of World War II my husband Ernest has been compiling material relating to his Peyton ancestors and their encounters with the native Indians of Newfoundland, the Beothuk. For forty years he has researched his family history and has recorded the contributions made by his ancestors to the history of Newfoundland.

As a sports-loving young man Ernest was not interested in such things. The war changed him into a person to whom home, and roots, meant a great deal. When one defends one's country, one seeks to know what the country stands for; and much of Newfoundland's early history had been only spottily recorded.

Ernest was interested to find that his great-grandfather, John Peyton "The Elder," the first member of the Peyton family to set foot in the New World, came to Newfoundland with Captain George Cartwright. This venture to an unknown land began with two summers on the coast of Labrador, starting in 1770. In 1772 he spent some time on the uncolonized northeast coast of Newfoundland. The lives of John Peyton and of his son John Peyton Jr., also known as John Peyton "The Younger," became part of Newfoundland history as these two men had many encounters with the Beothuk Indians, who were the native island race of Indians, and who became extinct with the death of Shanawdithit in 1829.

Many stories have been written about the Beothuk Indians and the early colonizers of the island of Newfoundland. It was Ernest's intention to explore the relationships of his ancestors to these native people, and try to put the history of his family in the proper perspective. Many unkind things had been said, and many accusations had been made and repeated over the years. Ernest had researched the facts, and kept the records. I began my work, and hope that in this book we can put matters to rest, and forever set the record straight on John Peyton the Elder and John Peyton the Younger. Because of their long involvement with the Exploits River, where they were granted salmon fishing rights by the English Government, I decided to call the book *River Lords: Father and Son.*

I hope the reader will find it an interesting story.

INTRODUCTION

Much has been written about our early settlers of Newfoundland, those who helped form our destiny. They did what was thought to be necessary in their day to accomplish their aim. Many suffered privations and loneliness, as well as confrontations with the native Beothuk Indians.

The Peyton entrepreneurs, father and son, were two such early settlers. They carried on a business of fur trapping and salmon fishing on the Exploits River in the eighteenth and nineteenth centuries.

How they began is a long story. It must start with the story of those who preceded them...

This book is dedicated to my husband Ernest,
a direct descendant of "Father and Son."

Softly on the forest floor,
Tread of moccasins, no more
Can glide through dale and hill.
Tho' tears may fall and we deplore
Their disappearance, and abhor
What causes man to kill.
How hard for us to contemplate
That wiped away a people's fate.

[Excerpt from a poem by Ernest A. Peyton]

1

The Beothuks

The Beothuk were an aboriginal tribe of Indians, native only to the island of Newfoundland. They were also called the Red Indians, from the manner in which these natives smeared their faces and bodies and sometimes even their clothing with red ochre. This red ochre was found in areas covering a certain type of slate rock. Dispersed throughout this type of slate was an oxide of iron that formed a peroxide when exposed to the surface; it was red in colour and powdery in form.[1] The purpose of its use by the Indians has not been fully understood—whether to ward off mosquitoes (gallinippers), evil spirits, or just used as a tribal ritual.

There is no mention of these natives by John Cabot when he discovered the island of Newfoundland in 1497, but the following year when he returned to the island he captured three of them and transported them to England, where they were presented to King Henry VII as public spectacles. According to *Kerr's Travels of 1498*, of this event:

> This year were also brought unto the King, three men taken in the Newfound-land...clothed with beast's skins and ate raw flesh and

spoke a language that no man could understand, in their
demeanor like to brute beasts...[2]

Another chronicler of world events wrote in his annals
four years later:

It is granted natives of North America in their wild attire were
exhibited to the public wonder of England in 1502.[3]

Many French vessels that frequented the island of
Newfoundland were also known to have captured several of
these natives and transported them to France. A chronicler of
the times named Charlevoix wrote of savages from the northeast coast having been brought to France in 1508. "There is no
profit at all to be obtained from these natives, who are the most
intractable of men, and one despairs of taming them."[4]

In 1509, the next year, six natives, referred to as savages,
were taken by the French ship *Bonaventure* and transported to
Rouen, France, along with their canoes, bow and arrows and
deerskin clothing.[5]

Two hundred and fifty-seven years later Sir Hugh Palliser, a
naval governor of Newfoundland, gave an account of these native
Indians to the British Admiralty in October 1766. He described
them as "a number of wild, ungovernable people from the interi-
or of Newfoundland, who are in every respect as savage and bar-
barous as the most savage tribes of the American continent."[6]

John August, a Beothuk, lived twenty years in captivity,
knowing no way of life other than the white man's. As an
infant he was rescued from his slain mother's papoose pouch in

August 1768. He was taken to England and exposed to the curiosity of the rabble at Poole for a two-penny piece.[7] When he was returned to Newfoundland he lived as a servant of Jeffrey G. Street at Trinity. When he died there he was interred by Street in a churchyard at Trinity; the burial was properly registered by the church.[8]

It is difficult to imagine how many similar such events may have taken place in the ensuing decades, building up a distrust and fear amongst the natives. For approximately two hundred and fifty years after the island's discovery it experienced an era of chaotic times. It was a no man's land, with neither law nor order. The surrounding waters were frequented by English West Country fishermen and European fishing boats, mostly French, and even some bona fide pirates. These fearless and daring men fished, traded and plundered, recklessly ignoring the rights of the native aborigines whose territory they had invaded. It is not surprising that the natives became hostile to the visitors from across the sea.

The hostility worked both ways; the natives were portrayed as savage, brutal and revengeful people, a people to be greatly feared. The Beothuk revenge took violent form in the beheading of their enemies; when news of these acts spread, the white man's fear grew. The Beothuk sometimes killed white men and cut off their heads to be placed on poles. If they came across the grave of a white man, their practice was to drive a stake down through it.[9]

For almost two and a half centuries these natives were ill-treated and considered a great inconvenience to the weak attempts at colonization. The early settlers, first on the Avalon Peninsula and then along the northeast coast, caused the few remaining members of the tribe to retreat farther into the interior of Newfoundland.

Then came the Mi'kmaq, the tribes of Indians crossing to the island from Cape Breton and Labrador. There were two Mi'kmaq tribes, the Shaunamuncs (Montagnais from Labrador), a friendly tribe, and the Shannocs (from Cape Breton), a tribe hated and feared by the Beothuk.[10] The Mi'kmaq were offered bounties by the French for Beothuk heads,[11] and many of them were equipped and experienced in the use of firearms. The Beothuk's defensive weapon was the bow and arrow, effective in an ambush, but no match for the power of a musket.

By the late 1700s the Beothuk tribe, now dwindling greatly, was hemmed between the two, the settlers along the northeast coast and the Mi'kmaq toward the west. This caused the remnants of the Beothuk tribe to make the area of the mighty Exploits River headwaters a final retreat. The shores of the "great lake," Red Indian Lake,[12] became the site of their winter encampments, in close proximity to caribou herds, a vital source of meat and furs.

During the summer months the Beothuk migrated to the northeast seacoast via the great Exploits waterway to Notre Dame Bay. This river and bay abounded with their favourite foods of salmon, trout, wild aquatic fowl and their eggs, and mussels and clams.

The English and French migratory fishing crews were also attracted to this same bay by the abundance of salmon and cod.

These two nationalities were continually in confrontation with each other and with the Red Indians. The French considered the Beothuk and the English their mortal enemies.

After years of spasmodic rule and untold atrocities to the Beothuk, something had to be done, and quickly, if the few remaining members of the tribe were to be reconciled and saved from extinction.

Cartwright, Buchan, Peyton Jr., Glascock, Cull and Cormack were unsuccessful in attempts to establish friendly relations with the tribe, but Peyton Jr. came closest to success. Had he been helped with further expeditions and more men, as he requested, he might have been spared the sorrow of seeing a native people wiped off the face of the earth.

After years of interference disrupting the tribe's living patterns through struggles, confrontations and finally starvation, the Beothuk tribe dwindled in numbers. The white man's aggressive colonialism drove them farther into the interior. Eventually the Beothuk race became extinct.

Judge Prowse wrote:

Whatever our sentimental feelings may be for those primitive inhabitants, all our history shows that one ineradicable feature in their [Beothuk] character was an insatiable hatred of the pale faces.[13]

2

Early English Settlers of Notre Dame Bay

The French and English fishermen of Newfoundland had settled many differences by treaty in 1713, giving fishing rights to the French along the eastern shore of the Northern Peninsula, known as the "French Shore." The English were given the fishing rights to the island-studded great bay of Notre Dame.

This beautiful bay with its principal large islands of Toulinguet (Twillingate), Fougue (Fogo), Change Islands, New World Island and Exploits Burnt Island, offered excellent opportunities for the new settlers, with the prime cod fishing grounds, where the English arrivals could establish fishing headquarters.

The shorelines of these islands provided ample space for the "planters"[14] to build fishing stages and fish-drying flakes. At first it was customary for these English West Country fishermen to spend only their summers in this new land and return to their homes in the fall. After the mid-1700s many brought their families and braved the isolation and long desolate winters. The islands of this bay offered some measure of protection from Beothuk intervention for the early settlers' families. Perhaps for this reason the islands of the bay were settled first.

Many sailing ships, after a long and difficult voyage across the Atlantic, would reach land on Fogo island, the most easterly point, to unload their human cargo of early pioneers. These settlers assembled here before moving farther on in quest of land and opportunity. Fogo became a "fulcrum" point, a stepping stone, for settlers of the northeast coast.

The earliest settlers of Twillingate were Tizzard, Smith, Moors, Bath and Young. Exploits Burnt Island was first settled by the Manuels from Exeter and the Jersey Islands, and the Seviours and Budgells from England. The first settlers at Fortune Harbour were John Dalton, Valentine Mahaney and Perry. James Wells, an Englishman, first settled at Leading Tickles or Rowsell's Island. (All four of these families later resettled at Exploits Burnt Island.)[15]

The few early pioneers who dared to dwell in tilts (makeshift log shelters) on and around the banks of the rivers on the main island of Newfoundland, for the purpose of salmon catching and fur trapping, lived lives of continuous fear and hardship. This was especially true of those who dwelt on the banks of the river Exploits, where the remnants of the Beothuk tribe had congregated. The new settlers knew little of their new country or of its native inhabitants, the Red Indians, that they were to encounter.

The staple foods of the early English settlers of this area were salt pork, hardtack biscuits and tea, which had to be supplemented by fish, game and the natural vegetation of the land. It was difficult to avoid fatigue and starvation. These men needed to be ingenious hunters, capable of augmenting the meagre food supplies with whatever wild game was available. For the early fur trappers it meant survival of the fittest, especially for those who dared to venture into unknown territory. In order to set up their traplines they blazed perilous trails, fighting the forces of nature, into an uncharted land of dense forest, barrens and, sometimes, treacherous muskeg.

During the late eighteenth century, squatters' rights, coupled with courage and aggressiveness, were essential to hold a river claim. At the end of the century it became law to place "an English youngster" on the Newfoundland salmon rivers and large streams in order for a claim to hold good.

These young men were usually assigned to this task in the early part of their servitude as apprentices. They were brought out from England in the early spring each year expressly for this purpose, to be the first squatters on the salmon rivers and brooks and thereby "copper-fasten" a claim.

The plentiful supply of salmon in the rivers in those early times was caught by using "rack work" across narrow, shallow channels of the rivers and large brooks. This was accomplished by building a weir or dam to divert the stream. The weir was constructed by driving stakes into the riverbed, similar to a fence, intertwining these with brushwood, thus diverting the main stream and school of salmon to the narrow opening where a "rack" or "toothed bar" would allow the flow of water through but block the passage of the salmon. This congregation of salmon in the dammed shallow pool allowed easy access for someone to dip them from the weir. It was not unusual to dip approximately 250 to 300 pounds of salmon in one hour.[16] The catch was then cleaned and pickled and shipped in tierces (casks of forty-two-gallon capacity and containing up to 300 pounds of pickled salmon) for export to England.

William Elliot was an early trapper in the area of Gander Bay Pond for thirty winters during the early 1800s. He would come to the water-side of Gander Bay to spend Christmas and return to his traplines until spring. The smallest number of pelts taken by Mr. Elliot was documented as being "thirty dozen Marten cats, besides Beaver and Otter."[17]

Another early trapper, Thomas Dicks of Indian Brook, carved "T.D. 1778" on a pine tree at Indian Pond. It was plainly seen by Thomas Peyton's surveyors in 1908.[18]

The first five men who attempted settlement at Grand Bay were killed by Beothuks. A crew arriving from Twillingate shortly afterwards found the dead bodies had been beheaded and the heads placed upon poles. One of the men killed was Captain Hall; hence, the bay was renamed Hall's Bay.[19]

Matthew Ward was the first settler in New Bay. He carried on a salmon fishery on the South West Brook and West Brook of New Bay.[20] Ward protected the salmon fishing rights for Squire Childe, who may have been a descendant of Sir Josiah Childe, who had trade interests in Newfoundland in the late 1600s and whose *New Discourse on Trade* was published in 1694.

Henry Rowsell was a former servant of Squire Childe and was believed to be a father to George and Thomas Rowsell; all three Rowsells, along with William Hooper, worked these brooks for Matthew Ward.

George and Thomas Rowsell frequently came in contact with the Beothuk and were well known by them. The Indians trusted George, but Thomas became their deadly enemy. According to Reverend W. Wilson in *Newfoundland and its Missionaries,* "[Thomas] was reputed as being a great Indian Killer.... He never went anywhere without his long flintlock gun, and woe betide the unfortunate Beothuk who dared to show himself where Rowsell was.... He is said never to have spared one of the natives."[21]

These stories, relayed many years later, may give doubt as to their veracity. However, it is a recorded fact that the Beothuk sought their revenge on their enemy. They caught Thomas Rowsell off guard while dipping salmon from his weir at South West Brook. He was ambushed, murdered, and in Beothuk fashion, was beheaded, stripped of clothing and his body pierced with arrows.[22]

Thomas Peyton, Justice of the Peace, wrote later:

Thomas Rowsell was killed by the Indians in 1789. It was on the South West Brook where Mr. Joseph Phillip has his sawmills. After it was discovered that Thomas Rowsell was killed at the South West Brook of New Bay by the Indians, his friends went in search of them and found two wigwams in what is now called Moors Cove. The Indians were away at the time. There was a house cat in one of the wigwams painted with red ochre. The cat appeared so nervous, so much so that the men were afraid to go into the wigwam. These men waited until nightfall, and when the Indians came home they came through what is now called Shoal Tickle. As soon as they came within a short gunshot, the men who were concealed away behind some rocks, discharged their guns loaded with buckshot, right into the two canoes as the Indians were returning to their homes. Most likely the Indians had been out on the islands[23] taking birds. It was never known how many were killed as the canoe drifted away.[24]

Captain Pulling was sent to the area the following year, 1790, to gather data of the incident from fishermen and trappers. Pulling's conclusion was "...Matthew Ward who was Thomas Rowsell's master is a notorious enemy of those unenlightened mortals and if he has not been the death of many of them he's much belyed [sic]."[25] Captain Pulling also reported "Rowsell's buckles were found hanging up in one of the Indian wigwams, tied to some of his buttons, by Thomas Taylor, Hooper and the rest when they went up the brook the ensuing winter."[26]

After Rowsell's death, his brother George assumed charge of the salmon stations and bought out the fishing rights from Matthew Ward for the sum of £90 sterling. Ward returned to England.[27]

From 1790 onwards the Rowsell enterprise became an extensive one, for, according to Messrs. Gundry of Bridport, England, a firm dealing in fishing nets, lines and cordage, the accounts of Rowsell's were fairly large ones, amounting in some cases to £1,000 yearly.[28]

When Henry Rowsell Sr. died at Hall's Bay at the age of ninety-three years, his body was carried to Nipper's Harbour for burial, "as his friends feared if he was buried at Hall's Bay at that time the Indians may take his body up."[29]

After George Rowsell died, his son Joseph operated the salmon post at South West Brook for forty-eight years when it was taken over by George's grandson Henry II. It was still being run by the Rowsells a hundred years after Thomas Rowsell's death.[30]

The Rowsells first settled at Leading Tickles, Sop's Arm and the Southwest Arm of New Bay.*

The Rowsells were also fur trappers in the New Bay area. Captain Buchan mentions them in his journal of 1810-1811. He came upon a trap bearing the Rowsell name while on his winter journey on foot into Newfoundland's interior.

Edward Gates was an early settler who fished the Loon Bay River and Jumper's Brook near Birchy Bay. During that time the Beothuk frequented their favourite summer haunts at what became Dildo Run and Reach Run nearby. While at Jumper's Brook, Gates was pierced in the throat by an arrow. Disheartened by the hostility of the Indians, he packed up and left the area, selling his fishery rights to William Andrews of Twillingate, who never took possession of the claim.[31]

Another early settler named Blake settled on the Indian Arm River for a short time. The next major owner of the fishing rights was Garland and Company, a mercantile firm of Fogo. One of Garland's bookkeepers, John Guinn, a well-educated man from Christchurch, Hampshire, England, then settled there in 1816 and carried on the salmon fishery. He was

---

* Ruth Rowsell of Leading Tickles, believed to have been the granddaughter of Thomas Rowsell, married Captain Samuel Stuckless of Twillingate, my maternal great-grandfather, in the early 1800s. He was a sea captain engaged by the mercantile firm of Edwin Duder Ltd.

When I was young, my mother often related to me the story handed down to her of how the Beothuks dared to get close to Thomas Rowsell and tease him. They came so close as to peer through the chinks (seams) of his log hut at night, taunting and calling, "Tom Rouse, Tom Rouse." A.L.P.

always on friendly terms with the Beothuk who frequented the area. Oftentimes an Indian would run out on Guinn's rack work which stretched across the river and spear a salmon and go "back again as quick as a wink." The Indians never attempted to injure Guinn, but occasionally he would miss a piece of rope or some small article which he supposed they had taken.[32]

Guinn had a set time for taking his rack work out of the river, regardless of his catch, and this policy was rigidly adhered to for conservation purposes. His average summer catch ranged from fifty-five to sixty tierces. When the fishery warden visited him in 1872 Guinn commented, "You, sir, may live to see the day when Indian Brook will not average ten."[33] The fishing rights of this brook were later sold to another settler name Joseph Harnett.

John Curtice established a sawmill between Loon Bay and Indian Arm. Several families settled on the north side of the Arm in connection with work at the sawmill.

Gander Bay River was first occupied by a MacBrior who later sold his salmon fishing rights in 1805 to Garland and Company of Fogo. As well, this firm held the rights to Dog Bay Brook or Dog Creek. Twelve years later, in 1817, this company sold its rights to George Hodder and Peter Rook, two former servants. Both men were illiterate, and confusion arose in their trading transactions, so they requested an educated "English youngster" to keep matters straight. John Bussie was sent from England for this purpose and later settled there. Hodder and Rook later dissolved the partnership and the rights were retained by Hodder.[34]

In 1822, Garland and Company sold their right and title of the Gander Bay River to two settlers, Hodder and Gillingham, two former servants of the company, Gillingham acting as boss. As many as seven hundred to eight hundred tierces of salmon had been taken there in one season. The pickling of the salmon was carried on at Salt Island.[35]

Although there was so much activity on the island it was not unusual for the Beothuks to cut the Englishmen's boats adrift from their moorings.

This small island lies in close proximity to the present Gander Bay bridge and contains an old burial ground. One tombstone bears the name of Gillingham who died in 1812, aged nineteen years; no doubt he was once a "youngster guardian" of the river.

There was another small island near the south bank of the Exploits River, close to the first "rattle" or "rapid" about a half-mile below the Bishop's Falls. During the early 1800s the salmon fishermen employed by Miller and Peyton camped on this island while attempting to build rack work and a weir from island to riverbank. Although it meant considerable time and hard work to anchor such a weir with ballast, exceptional catches were taken up, up to three hundred pounds every hour. However, after only twenty-four hours, the swollen river, flooded by heavy rain, swept it all away. The men soon realized it was folly to try and tame this turbulent river, and the small island became known as Folly Island.

As bountiful as the salmon catches were, on only one known occasion, in 1872, did the Gander Bay River beat the great and mighty River Exploits.

3

The Exploits River
and Its Pioneers

...the brimming river,
For men may come and men may go,
But I go on forever.

LORD ALFRED TENNYSON

The Exploits River, approximately two hundred miles in length, originates from the southern part of the Long Range Mountains with many tributaries and large brooks flowing into its system. Almost in the middle of its course it expands into Red Indian Lake, thirty-six miles long, and in places three miles wide. Its mighty flow of water rushes and tumbles, cascading toward the sea, finally discharging into Exploits Bay, a southern arm of Notre Dame Bay. On reaching its mouth its turbulence ends, its fury spent, as if Alpheus, the river God, "flows its waters under the sea to mingle quietly with nymphs."[36]

It was once an untamed, uncharted waterway of strong currents, fast-flowing rapids and several cascading waterfalls, pass-

15

ing through prime forest and picturesque unbounded wilderness of prime Beothuk territory. The river and its boundaries became the final habitat and retreat of the Beothuk people. Flowing from the interior of Newfoundland toward the northeast coast, the river became the Indian's chief natural highway. Not only was it the aborigines' natural "way out" to the seacoast, but the early pioneers' natural "way in" to the heart of Beothuk land.

In the wintertime the frozen river was transformed into accessible footpaths of ice, creating a corridor whereby the white men could travel farther inland to trap fur-bearing animals, a valuable resource.

In attempts to establish contact with the Indians and achieve some kind of reconciliation with them, many journeys were made on the Exploits River. The first was by Lieutenant John Cartwright in 1768, then William Cull in 1809, Captain David Buchan in 1810–11, John Peyton Jr. and his elderly father John Sr. in March 1819, Captain William Nugent Glascock in the summer of 1819, Captain David Buchan in January of 1820 and William Epps Cormack in the fall of 1827.

Cartwright, Buchan, Glascock and Cormack spent only a fleeting time on the Exploits River in the attempts they made to encounter the Beothuk. They and their men found the going too rough. Their efforts were futile.

Many men came and went but the Peytons, father and son, stayed on. They settled on its banks and there lived out their lives. They were pioneers, filled with determination to overcome the many difficulties, and they held the salmon fishing rights of the river for a total of seventy-nine years.

The early pioneers had much to contend with to brave the Exploits River boundaries. Dense forests to the shorelines were forbidding and oppressive. In summer the myriads of devouring black flies, mosquitoes and sand flies were a torturous ordeal. The presence of the hungry wolf (now extinct on the island) was another deterrent to the adventurer.

Yet the Exploits River had much to offer. Its waters abounded with salmon, on its shores nested copious numbers of waterfowl and its surrounding forests contained fur-bearing animals in abundance. A small number of men felt it was worth facing the discomforts and hazards of such a country, and mid-1700s they attempted to settle on the banks of the Exploits River.

At that time two Englishmen, Hodge and Hollett, stepped ashore on the sandbar that jutted out from land on the south side of the Exploits River estuary. This sandbar was named Lower Sandy Point (the location of the present-day Lawrenceton). They were the first known pioneers to attempt to settle on the banks of the river. Their intention was to set up a salmon fishery. They were also trappers and their trapping area (principally for beaver, otter and "Marten cat") was to the back of Northern Arm. The mountain range of Hodge's Hills was named after one of them.[37]

John Cousens was an early "planter" who is believed to have settled on the northern side of the river estuary as early as the 1760s. He was one of the party that accompanied Lieutenant John Cartwright and his brother George on their trek to Lieutenant's Lake (now Red Indian Lake) in 1768.[38]

The exact length of Hodge and Hollett's stay and that of John Cousens on the river is uncertain, nor is it known why their ventures were abandoned. The fishing rights on the river were taken over by Harry Miller around 1770, at first with the help of two men, Thomas Taylor and Jack Hooper.

Harry Miller, a native of Wimborne, near Christchurch, England, had been living at Fogo, and carrying on a cod fishery. Thomas Taylor, at first in partnership with Miller, became Miller's boss on the Exploits River. Jack Hooper, a deaf-mute, thoughtlessly referred to as Dumb Jack, was an apprentice and a brother to William Hooper, apprenticed to Matthew Ward of New Bay.

Although the salmon fishing headquarters was on the south side of the Exploits River mouth at Lower Sandy Point, Miller had a dwelling constructed on the north shore, farther out into the bay, about nine miles from Charles Brook. Thomas Taylor's salmon station, also on the north side of the river, was just below the Nut Islands (four in number, a mile below the first "rattle" or small waterfall), and the station became known as Thomas Taylor's Point.

As time went by several more men were apprenticed to Harry Miller, and he commanded twelve salmon fishing stations along a thirty-mile stretch of the Exploits River and on the large adjoining streams. Miller's enterprise was a considerable and profitable venture, although he was faced with many adversities. His control of the Exploits River earned him the title "major-domo" or principal man.

He had several salmon stations on the Great Rattling Brook tended by Richard Richmond, Nicholas Eton and James

Lily. Tilts (log shelters) were constructed as far as forty miles inland on this stream. William Richmond, a brother of Richard, fished at another of Miller's salmon stations, twelve miles up the Exploits River. William Cull also fished and trapped for Miller at Northern and Peter's Brooks on the north shore. Pike (believed to have been James Pike) operated Miller's cooperage at Lower Sandy Point, producing kegs, barrels, hogsheads and tierces. As the cooperage was formerly owned and operated by Hodge and Hollett, all cooperage gear carried the brand of H.H.

Other men apprenticed to and employed by Miller were John Morris, Matthew Hughster, Maurice Cull, James Green, James Brown, John Day, John Boles, Humphrey Coles, John Snelgrove (also known as Jackie Jones), Butler and Carey. These men pursued two careers as salmon catchers and fur trappers.

Many of these young English apprentices left behind their homes and families to learn a trade and seek a new and independent life in a new land. If they were seeking adventure, they surely found it. Their houses were individual tilts, makeshift shelters built entirely of logs, the seams or chinks ("chinkers") stuffed or "stoged" with sphagnum moss to block the drafts and keep out the weather. These tilts were built about ten miles apart, on either side of the riverbanks and on the banks of tributary streams, for the sole purpose of commercial salmon fishing and fur trapping.

These men lived lonely lives, seeing few people and expecting no one, except the Indians often noticed slipping by outside. They were attracted to the gear left outside the white men's tilts. Equipment such as ropes, axes or kettles would often be carried away by the natives. The only path these Englishmen knew were the overgrown shorelines of the riverbanks, the trails of the caribou leading to Beothuk deer fences[39] and the narrow footpaths of the Beothuk through the almost impenetrable underbrush. The quietness of the wilderness sometimes shattered by a loon's cry must have been unnerving. A dog was a good companion to some, but others had only their "fowling piece" or long flintlock musket. It was vital to carry a gun wherever they went to obtain their day's food supply. The rations, consisting of the staple foodstuffs, had to be supplemented with wild fowl and game.

However, the frugal living conditions did not cause them to stray entirely from conventional living, for on Sundays it was customary to roast a beaver. Roasted beaver, especially a young animal, resembled quite closely roast lamb in flavour and texture. It was the nearest these Englishmen could find in this new wilderness to the familiar "tastes of mutton and ale."

Around 1775, with many men in his employ and an expanding business of exporting furs, skins and pickled salmon for the lucrative London market, Harry Miller took into partnership a younger Englishman who was a native of his hometown of Wimborne. His name was John Peyton.

4

John Peyton
(Later Known as John the Elder)

They dared beyond their strength,
hazarded beyond their judgement,
and in extremities were of excellent hope.

THUCYDIDES

The surname Peyton can be traced back to the eleventh century in England. The name was adopted by the deMalets of France when they crossed over from Normandy in the time of William the Conqueror. The first deMalet accepted the name dePeyton from the manor of Peyton Hall in Suffolk. The name was later changed to Peyton.[40] It is also one of the earliest names connected with the colonization of Virginia, U.S.A.[41]

John Peyton (later to be referred to as John the Elder) was born at Wimborne, Christchurch, Hampshire, England in 1747. He was one of the earliest river lords, a pioneer of the River Exploits. He was twenty-three years of age when he made his first journey to the New World in 1770. He lived most of the rest of his life on the banks of the Exploits. He died on the riverbank fifty-seven years later.

Peyton journeyed to Newfoundland in company with George Cartwright.[42] On the way to Labrador, Cartwright's sailing schooner *Nimrod* put in, as was customary, to the first point of land, the island of Fogo on July 7, 1770. While at Fogo the sailing schooner *Enterprise*, owned by Coghlan and Lucas, was engaged for the continuation of the journey to the trading post in Labrador, where Mr. Lucas intended to explore the Labrador coastline to the northward.

During the waiting period while the *Enterprise* was being fitted for the Labrador voyage, George Cartwright engaged a sloop to take his party on a cruise into Exploits Bay in search of the Beothuk. Although Cartwright does not mention Peyton in his journal, Thomas Peyton frequently referred in his journal of the trip his grandfather John Peyton made with Cartwright up the Exploits River in search of the natives.

This is the first encounter with the territory of the Beothuk that Peyton experienced, and his first encounter with the Bay of Exploits and its turbulent river. It was during this stopover at Fogo that John Peyton met Harry Miller.

After serving two summers with Cartwright on the coast of Labrador, Peyton returned to Fogo and, settling there, he carried on a cod fishery for several years, having had some experience with the fisheries in the Channel Islands.

At this time, Harry Miller had resettled on the Exploits River where he was carrying on his extensive salmon fishery and fur-trapping trade. Around 1775, Peyton left Fogo and moved to the Exploits River, in partnership with Harry Miller and James Bown. On a will drawn up by Harry Miller and witnessed by Thomas Taylor in late 1775, mention is made of this triple partnership.[43] Harry Miller's handwritten will reads:

> NOV. 1775
> This is my last will and power, for to obstruct and cut off all others, before written or shall be written hereafter. I do hereby authorize and empower John Peaton [sic] and James Bown, if that it should please the Almighty to take me from this transitory life, to take my wareing[44] cloths[45] craft[46] and all other things belonging to me, for their own and no one to control them. Which is given from under my hand, the 21st day of November, 1775.
>
> By me, Harry Miller, Witness John Irish
> and his Thomas X Taylor
> mark

Peyton, who was then twenty-eight years of age, took up his duties on the river and tended the salmon fishing station at Upper Sandy Point. This sandbar jutted well out into the river mouth on the north side, in the vicinity of the extreme end of the settlement now known as Peterview.

It is uncertain what became of James Bown, whether he returned to England or died, for in the intervening twenty-five years the enterprise was only known as belonging to Miller and Peyton.

Over the next few years John Peyton generally returned to England during the winter months. In England he was a member of the Masonic Lodge and belonged to Hengist Lodge #195 of Christchurch.[47]

The date is not known, but while in England Peyton married Anne Galton and resided at Wimborne. It is believed that he married late in life when he was in his forties. They had three children: John Jr., Susan, and James. John Peyton was forty-six years of age when his son John Jr. was born.

Travelling the Atlantic by sailing ship each spring and fall proved to be unrewarding. John Peyton decided to settle in Newfoundland. He chose for himself a permanent location on the banks of the Exploits River estuary at Upper Sandy Point. The house was described as "a very pleasant comfortable house...having an excellent garden behind, with a grass plot and a few scattered birch trees between it and the river in front, and altogether, a very pretty-looking and quite an English sort of place."[48]

Peyton probably had intentions of bringing his wife and young family from England to settle in his newly built home, but probably Anne Peyton balked at the idea. Very few homes were being built on the mainland off the northeast coast of Newfoundland before the turn of the nineteenth century.

The earliest settlers, seeking refuge from Beothuk interference, chose to live on the islands of the bays. Those who did settle on the islands experienced many difficulties as they braved the isolation and harsh winters.

As Miller and Peyton continued their pursuits in the Bay of Exploits, they competed with the Beothuk for the resources of the river and surrounding areas. Their dealings with the Beothuk were often criticized. Influenced by George Cartwright's success on trading with the Esquimaux, natives of Labrador, Peyton may have hoped for the same possibilities of trade with the Newfoundland natives. However, he was unsuccessful in establishing better relations with the Beothuk. They had long since rejected the white man's ways.

The Indian tribe considered the white man's possessions as fair game, and the white men were forced by necessity to retrieve their vital traps and nets. Furs, that had taken months for the Peyton and Miller crews to trap, were often stolen by the Beothuks. Some were recovered, and often Beothuk furs and skins were taken in retaliation by the Peyton and Miller crews in "tit for tat" fashion. Confrontations were frequent and did not put Peyton and Miller or their men on a friendly footing with members of the Indian tribe. These men were well known by the Beothuk and feared by them.

John Peyton the Elder was as hard as any old warrior in times when the going was extremely rough. Accounts of those times, though sketchy, portray him as a merciless man unsympathetic towards the Beothuk. His supremacy over the river naturally aroused much resentment in the few remaining members of the tribe. His presence was a blatant intrusion on their domain.

Magistrate Bland of Bonavista, although receiving his information second-hand from a Mr. Slater of Fogo, criticized Peyton's attitude towards the natives and reported in 1790 that "Peyton had rendered himself infamous for his persecution of the Indians" and suggested that it would be a good idea "to expel him from the Bay of Exploits."[49]

Captain Pulling was sent to the Bay of Exploits in August 1792 to investigate and make a report on the conduct of the settlers towards the Beothuk. Peyton was not there at the time,

but with his family in England. Pulling gleaned from the trappers stories of Peyton's behaviour. No doubt the tales were
embellished, but they portrayed him as merciless and cruel. He
undoubtedly was to ensure his own survival and that of his
enterprise. Pulling noted his absence from the river at the time,
saying "Peyton now resides at Christchurch in England, having
made his fortune."[50]

This appears to have been very unlikely, as he returned
again and again for many more years.

Harry Miller died in 1800. Peyton had bought shares in the
firm and now inherited full rights to the salmon fishery and
properties on the river.

The confrontation with the natives, previously ignored,
were becoming a worry to the authorities at the beginning of
the nineteenth century. The white man's conscience was beginning to bother him in his dealings with the natives.

In the summer of 1810, the Newfoundland governor, Sir
Thomas Duckworth, realizing that the native Indian tribe was
dwindling rapidly, issued a proclamation to all the inhabitants
of the island, warning them to live on friendly terms with the
Beothuk. At the same time, a reward of £100 was offered by
the government to anyone who could bring about and establish
a relationship of goodwill with these natives.

It was felt that to capture one or several and appease them
with gifts of trinkets and other presents, then return them to
their tribe, would probably bring about a desired reconciliation.

By now Peyton was in his sixties. The hard life was beginning to be too much for him. He needed a young man to help

him carry out the duties of his Exploits River endeavour. John Peyton Jr. was living in England, strong and healthy, educated and assertive, a likely successor if only he could be persuaded to join his father.

The elder Peyton made yet another voyage to England in the fall of 1811. In the spring of 1812, his wife was still unwilling to share the rugged life led by her husband in Newfoundland and remained in England. This time her husband returned to the New World accompanied by his son John Jr., who was prepared to accept the challenges of an uncolonized land.

The Wimborne Coat of Arms

Wimborne, the ancestral home of "Father and Son"

5

John Peyton the Younger

John Peyton Jr., like his father, was also born at Wimborne, near Christchurch, England, on August 31, 1792. He was baptized January 21, 1793, also at Wimborne. He was educated at Christchurch School. At the age of sixteen he entered the Imperial Government service and served with them for three years as a junior clerk at Somerset House, London, then the Navy pay office. At that time there were three hundred clerks employed in the office and around the docks.

When John and his father came to Newfoundland they journeyed across the Atlantic on a two-masted, square-rigged sailing brigantine of about a hundred tons belonging to John Slade, a wealthy merchant of Poole, England. The name of the sailing brig was the *John and Thomas*, but referred to, and later nicknamed the "Hammer and Tongs," from her habit of stopping at every big crest of a wave and pounding it to pieces before proceeding on. The *John and Thomas* was one of a fleet of sailing ships that brought cargo and supplies, as well as passengers, to Newfoundland. Slade owned approximately 150 such sailing vessels that plied the Newfoundland trade.

On this voyage in 1812, during the war between England and France, the brig was under a convoy of British men-o'-war. It was bound for the port of Fogo, carrying general fishing supplies for the business firm of Garland and Company. On reaching the Newfoundland coast it was released from convoy and touched in at the port of Carbonear before proceeding northward. The following excerpt is taken from the journal of Thomas Peyton, son of John Jr.:

> I often heard my father speak of his passage out to Newfoundland. Of course in a large fleet of Merchant vessels there would be a great difference in the sailing qualities of the same. If a very dull sailor [meaning a sailing ship] dropped astern, a gun would fire; the main topsail of the Commodore's ship would fall aback and each of the fleet would have to follow example. One of the Frigates would then have to tow the slower one up. The masters of these dull sailors hated to be towed and could be seen under full canvas, while most others were under short sail. Every evening at the proper time when the signal came from the Commodore, the Frigates would crowd on all sail and sail around the stragglers and whip them up into line. Signals were kept burning all night and a count would be made to see all was safe. After half passage out, the Masters of some of the smarter sailors [ships] got uneasy at the tedious work of jogging along and wished to get away from the convoy. Of course each vessel had her distinct flag and if the Commodore saw any forging ahead or edging away, a gun would be fired to draw attention. One or two of the more daring Captains, on two or three occasions, did not pay attention to the signals. After waiting a sufficient time, a puff of smoke could be seen from the bow of the Commodore's ship or one of the Frigates, followed by a sound of shot dancing over the water; the would be erstwhile vessel, as much as to say, "Do as I order you or I will soon stop you." After a long tedious voyage the fleet arrived on the coast of Newfoundland in the early part of June; the good ship *John and Thomas*, putting into the port of Carbonear. My father told me he walked ashore on the drift ice. Carbonear

was then a port of some importance. There were bretesse
[embattlements on both sides] works of several guns mounted as
a Battery.

He then gives the following description of the brigantine
John and Thomas:

She was built of English oak, fastened with the best of copper fastening and manned with British seamen. She was dry rigged, flush
deck; a rail running her sides on staunchins [sic], more for the purpose of fastening braces and placing belaying pins than anything
else. As bulwarks, a few boards nailed across the stern and on the
quarters, also a few boards nailed around the bow; all open amidships and all awash when a sea was running. I heard my father say
he used to watch for an opportunity to run from the quarter deck,
which was lifted out of the water, and perch on the windlass.

The cook on this voyage was a man named William Cox.
He later founded William Cox and Company and accumulated
considerable wealth.

The brig *John and Thomas* had on board this particular voy-
age of 1812 many young Englishmen apprenticed to the mer-
cantile houses and established "planters" of the new colony.
Amongst them were fourteen English youths to be assigned as
"youngsters"[51] to hold good the river claims on the Gander
River, Dog Creek (Dog Bay), Indian Arm River, Loon Bay
Brook, Exploits River and its five large tributaries (Little and
Great Rattling Brooks, Peter's Arm Brook and Jumper's Brook,
New Bay Brook, Sop's Arm Brook) and the three Hall's Bay
Brooks (Charles Brook, South West and West Brooks).
Nineteen-year-old John Peyton Jr. was the assignee "young-
ster" for the main stream of the Exploits.

After leaving Carbonear it took a considerable period of favourable winds and weather, along with dodging heavy ice floes along the coast, for the *John and Thomas* to reach Seldom-Come-By on the north side of Fogo island. Although it was late in June, the weather was cold. The damp easterly winds had jammed the heavy northern pack ice into the inlets and bays. The unaccustomed sight of a dazzling, white expanse of rough ice, reaching as far as the eye could see, awoke awe and fear amongst those who were about to face the challenge of going ashore. The bleak shorelines, where no houses were visible, had a forbidding look. To the fourteen adventurous English youths the outlook was desolate. However, it was customary for an apprentice to serve his master for six to eight years, and it was not considered manly to shirk one's duty.

Those young men who were to claim the salmon fishing rights for Garland and Company of Fogo, on the Gander Bay River, Dog Creek and Indian Arm Brook, disembarked at Fogo and "were marched away, over the heavy pack ice lying around the coast, to their charges."[52]

Those assigned to the Exploits River and points farther north "were forced to wait until the ice moved off the shore in order to travel into Exploits Bay by boat to their destinations."[53]

As the journey continued into Exploits Bay the waters became more sheltered and the ice floes loosened. The huge tracts of timberland, the impenetrable stands of fir, spruce and pine, where few white men had yet dared to tread, presented a forbidding aspect. Here was the refuge of the Beothuk natives, known to the Europeans as "savages."

A formidable challenge faced the newcomers, but they did not shrink from the prospect. They believed that they, as colonists for their mother country England, had a duty to civilize this new land and its native inhabitants. They were not alone; other parts of North America had undergone and were undergoing the same process. In their arrogance was no evil intent, merely the wish to prosper, and to bring honour to themselves and their country.

That the native Beothuk did not share this view was not a concern to these men, and in this, too, the river lords were typical of their time.

The youthful John Peyton was perhaps much luckier than other apprenticed "youngsters" on that voyage. He had the companionship of his father, and his living conditions on the Exploits were perhaps better than most at the time, for his father already had an impressive dwelling at Upper Sandy Point. From there John Jr. carried out his duties of patrolling the main stream of the Exploits and protecting the Peyton river claim.

The younger Peyton's sturdy physique and stamina were assets that helped him endure the hard life. The experiences he was to have while comparatively young were also valuable, preparing him for the time when he would become lord of the river.

When John first arrived at the Exploits River there was much exploring to be done in his newly adopted land. He discovered an old gun in one of the storehouses, of the old type, flint and steel, or as was known then as the open fireplace gun. Thomas Peyton, Justice of the Peace, later wrote in his journal:

> This gun barrel had the lock, such as it was, nailed on a rough stock. [My father] had it refitted in a modern way with a decent stock of the time; still flint and steel and used it to shoot ducks and geese, for which it proved valuable for its long range… Afterwards my father sent the barrel to Bemister and had it renovated and made into a percussion gun.

Bemister mentioned above was James Bemister, a first-class gunsmith then living at Christchurch, England. He later emigrated to Exploits and was employed by John Peyton Jr., engaged in the ironworks of the shipbuilding trade.

Thomas Peyton wrote, circa 1906:

> I used the same gun on being able to do so and have it still in my use. This gun barrel must now be nearly, if not quite, two hundred years old. It had branded on the stock H.H. for Hodge and Hollett, who were as far as is known the first settlers on the Exploits River.

John grew fond of his adopted land, especially the grandeur of the majestic River Exploits. He had a feel for nature and wildlife and he loved the freedom of the great outdoors. He become familiar with the river and its surrounding area. It was the heart of Beothuk land. He became knowledgeable of the ways of the Beothuk, learned of their habits, their behaviour patterns and their way of life as hunters. He was aware of the hazards he might have to encounter, yet his per-

spective differed from that of his father. He had a more benev-
olent attitude towards the natives and spoke of them "as his
fellow creatures." He wanted a reconciliation and understanding between the white man and the "Red Indians" and to see
both live peacefully side by side.

Still, the younger John, who came to this country forty-two
years after his father, has often been mistaken for the older man
in accounts of recent decades. This has caused many inaccura-
cies to have been stated as facts. Due to this mistaken identity,
John Jr. has been blamed for the actions and events which may
or may not have taken place during his father's time.

Apart from the Exploits River John traversed the small
brooks, used flat-bottom boats to portage from pond to pond,
visiting his various traplines. With his background of navigational knowledge acquired in the mother country, he became an
experienced boatman, able to use all crafts from the riverboat
to the sailing skiff and sailing schooner in the bays.

Thomas Peyton, when writing of his father John "the
Younger" said:

> My father being young and strong and healthy took a leading
> part in the life of a salmon catcher, trapper and hunter, and I was
> often told by the men who served with him that he never
> seemed so happy as he did when he was tramping through the
> snow on snowshoes with a bundle of steel traps slung up to his
> back and for some years [he] carried on in this business of trap-
> ping and furring with varied success, keeping a number of flat
> bottom boats at the lakes in the interior of the country to use
> in the spring and autumn months. The furs mostly caught or
> taken being beaver, otter, "marten cat," muskrat and weasel.
> These furs after my father came to this country were sent home
> and sold in the London market.

Before leaving England, John was received into Henist Masonic Lodge #195 of Christchurch (the same Lodge as his father). On March 2, 1813, he received his third-degree certificate from this fraternal order. The Masons were widely respected and John Jr. was a young man whose character was in good stead.

The law requiring a "youngster" for river claims was no longer compulsory after 1813. John, while still carrying out his duties on the Exploits River for the next several years, took a greater interest in his father's export trade. The elder John, having turned seventy years of age, was becoming more and more reliant on his son's help and new ideas. The son proposed plans that would expand the business to include the export of salt cod.

This island of Exploits in the mouth of Exploits Bay seemed an ideal location to start such a venture. It was situated in the midst of proven, prime cod fishing grounds and a comparatively safe distance from any possible Beothuk intervention. Several "planters" such as the Manuels, Seviours, Budgells and a few other English settlers had already established headquarters there, all in pursuit of the cod fishery.

Some community planning for the island had already been set in place. Blocks of land measuring eighty yards of shoreline and two hundred yards inwards were allotted each "planter" who was desirous of settling there.

The Register of Fishing Rooms for the Exploits Burnt Island, commenced in 1806, shows John Peyton Jr. holding a block of land in 1815 for a cod fishery premises. On it were built a house and store, a fishing stage and fish-drying flakes.

With John Jr.'s vision and foresight the business thrived, employing more men. John divided his time between the island and the river: the river during the spring and early summer salmon-fishing season, and Exploits Island during the mid-summer and fall cod fishery. Then they returned to the estuary and Upper Sandy Point, the winter residence, when the winter trapping season started.

The younger John took over the reins of the Peyton enter-prise from his father around 1815–16. He was then in his early twenties. Although all fishing rights and properties of the river enterprise were inherited by his father in 1800 from his partner Harry Miller as stated in the will of 1775, John Jr. wanted to make matters "right and proper," and wished to have the will probated.

This was done in 1815 as is evidenced by the following let-ter requested of Thomas Taylor, witness to the will:

Whereas Harry Miller of Exploits in the island of Newfoundland, planter, deceased. Executed of will bearing date the 21st day of November 1775 witnessed by John Irish and Thomas Taylor. And whereas it hath been represented to me that it would be attended with very great expense, should Thomas Taylor, the only surviving witness to the Execution of this said will be obliged to come to St. John's, to prove the due Execution thereof.

I do therefore by virtue of the power of authority in me vested, here-by authorize and appoint Andrew Pearce Esq. Of the island of Fogo, Justice of the Peace, to cause to appear before him the said Thomas Taylor concerning the due executor of the said will. And also to cause to appear before him and said Andrew Pearce Esq. such other witnesses as to him may appear necessary to prove the hand writing of them the deceased Harry Miller and John Irish.

> And I hereby direct that the said will together with the affi-
> davits made before him the said Andrew Pearce Esq. is proof of
> the due Execution of the said will be sent by the first safe
> opportunity under cover to me at St. John's.
> In witness whereof I have herewith set my hand and seal at
> St. John's, Newfoundland this 14th day of October 1815.
> By James Blaikie Esq., one of His Majesty's Justices of the
> Peace for the island of Newfoundland and Surrogate of the
> Probate Court of the said island appointed by Commission
> from the Honourable Caesar Colclough, Chief Justice of the
> said island who is gone to England for the establishment of his
> home.

The "servants" who had worked for John Peyton Sr. and
Harry Miller now were in the younger John's charge. Many of
the Englishmen employed by Miller and Peyton Sr. stayed on
with the firm for forty and fifty years. Some later married and
had children in Newfoundland; some of these names still exist.
The longest survivor of the group was John Snelgrove, also
called Jacky Jones. As an older, reliable servant he was for many
years retained by John Jr. and later by his son Thomas.

While still employing the old seasoned trappers and fishermen, John apprenticed several English youth, as was customary in those days, to work along with the older men.

Captain Richard Rogers, a family friend from Wimborne
and a close personal friend of John Jr., had emigrated to
Newfoundland and wanted his sons apprenticed to John to
learn a trade, thirteen-year-old George to become a mariner in
the cod fishery and Edward to gain experience in the fur trade.

The eight-year indenture of George Rogers, as a mariner
apprentice, was signed by George and his father on April 2,
1815 and reads as follows:

Indenture witnesseth that George Rogers aged 13 years, son of Richard Rogers of Christchurch in the County of Southampton, of his own free will and with the consent of his said father of Southampton, of his own free will doth put himself Apprentice to John Payton [sic], the younger of Christchurch aforesaid Mariner to learn his Art and with him after the manner of an apprentice to serve from the day of this date thereof unto the full end and term of eight years from thence next following to be fully complete and ended. During which term the said Apprentice, his Master faithfully shall serve, his secrets keep his lawful commands, everywhere gladly go, he shall do no damage to his said Master nor see to be done to others but to his power shall tell or forthwith give warning to his said Master of the same, he shall not waste the goods of his said Master nor lend them unlawfully to any. He shall not commit fornication nor contract matrimony within the said term. He shall not play cards or dice tables or any other unlawful games whereby his said Master may have any loss with his own good or others during the said term without license of his said Master. He shall neither buy or sell. He shall not haunt taverns or play houses nor absent himself from his said Master's service day or night unlawfully but in all things as a faithful apprentice. He shall behave himself towards his Master and all this during the said term with the said John Payton [sic] in consideration of such services doth hereby covenant and agree to and with the said Richard Rogers that he and his said Master, his said apprentice in the Art of a Mariner which he useth by the best means that he can shall teach and instruct or cause to be taught and instructed finding unto the said Apprentice sufficient meat, drink, wearing apparel, bedding, lodging and all other necessaries during the said term. And for the true performance of all and every the said Covenants and Agreements either of the said parties bindeth himself unto the other by these present in witness whereof the parties above named to these Indentures interchangeably have put their Hands and Seals, the twenty-seventh day of April and in the fifty-fifth year of the Reign of our Sovereign Lord George the third by the Grace of God of the United Kingdom of Great Britain and Ireland, King, Defender of the Faith and in the year of our Lord, one thousand eight hundred and fifteen.

Signed: George Rodgers, Richard Rogers and John Peyton Jr.

When George reached twenty-five years of age, four years after his eight-year apprenticeship had been served, he was drowned in a storm. John noted the sad event in his diary: "14th Sept., 1827: George Rodgers lost; supposed to have upset his boat. Phillip Shiner one of the crew."

Edward Rogers, while carrying out his trapping duties, had a close encounter with the Beothuk in 1817. The Indians, while carrying away fourteen of his "marten cat" traps that he had set, shot an arrow that pierced the roof of a bough house built over a trap to keep off the snow.[54]

In the early 1800s, Newfoundland was being ruled by naval governors, perhaps the most suitable government at the time for migratory fishermen. As the colony grew it strove to attain autonomy with a resident governor, its own courts and a Chief Justice. Justices of the Peace were appointed whenever possible, wherever the number of people in the area warranted it.

John Jr.'s intelligence, good schooling, steadfast character and three years service with the Imperial Government in England made him a good candidate for an appointment as a representative of justice.

Thomas Peyton was later to note this in his journal:

[My father] was appointed a Justice of the Peace for the Northern District of Newfoundland and the coast of Labrador in 1818. He received his first commission from Governor Sir Charles Hamilton. Both Sir Charles and Lady Hamilton were very friendly with him.

Justice of the Peace was a very prestigious appointment and an important one, as it carried with it a wide range of responsibilities.

The only mode of travel around the island of Newfoundland at that time was the sailing schooner. John needed transportation around the coastline to areas that came under his jurisdiction. He obtained a small sailing schooner for this purpose. He named this schooner the *Susan* for his only sister who had died earlier in England.

The need for fishing schooners and fishing boats in the Bay of Exploits soon became obvious. John saw the potential and started a shipyard on Exploits Island (the first such venture in Notre Dame Bay) and another shipyard later at Indian Point on the river estuary. It was for this particular reason that he acquired a second block of land in 1818, adjacent to the fishing premises he already owned on Exploits Burnt Island. The two premises were registered in 1818 in the list of Fishing Rooms as "bounded on one side by the fishing rooms of James Wells and on the southeast by a bald rock."

The port of Poole, near John's home at Wimborne, had already been for a century a supply centre for the Newfoundland trade. There was no shortage of craftsmen available in that area, especially those required for the task of shipbuilding.

Thomas Peyton noted in his journal:

Not only ship's carpenters but other tradesmen were at this time brought out from England, a wheelwright and blacksmiths; some had fought in the Peninsular War and [were] partly disabled. One in particular who fought in the battle received a musket ball under the ribs. His name was Robert Crabtree... I am aware that a first class gunsmith came out at that time; James Bemister of Christchurch. It was from these men that my father imported, that the native builders from Exploits and round about, got their first lessons in shipbuilding and many other

works. My father was the first to introduce shipbuilding in the
Notre Dame Bay.

Mr. Garrett Curtice, then living at Salmonier, St. Mary's
Bay, was brought to Exploits Island as superintendent of the
two shipyards. During the late fall of 1819 the first keel was
laid. This schooner John would name the *Anne*, for his mother.

6

Encounters with the Beothuks

As the Peyton business expanded there was a stepping-up of operations and activities around and about the Exploits River estuary and Exploits Bay. Naturally this caused some alarm amongst the Indians. They perceived the white men as invaders, edging more and more into their territory.

One of the aims of the natives was to disrupt the settlers' work and thereby discourage their activities; in this they hoped eventually to banish them from their domain. One Beothuk prank of great consequence to the settlers was to cut the fishermen's boats adrift from their moorings. This produced frustration amongst the owners, who were often left stranded.

John experienced two such incidents. The first occurred shortly after he started his cod fishery at Exploits Island in 1815. His fishing boat, and one belonging to George Luff of the same place, were cut loose during the night. Moveable items in the boats such as fishing tackle and canvas sails were carried away.[55]

John was fully aware of the Beothuk's summer expeditions down the Exploits River. He knew they were constantly on the lookout for a chance to take articles such as nets, traps, ropes and tackle, canvas sails, axes and knives.

But perhaps John was not aware of the mistrust and hostility that the Beothuk felt for his father and Harry Miller in the years past, due to the actions of the Miller and Peyton crews in retrieving their gear and furs.

Although the nightly visits of the Beothuk were an annoyance, the younger Peyton had not yet carried out any retaliatory measures. When his second boat was cut adrift by Beothuks, this time a much larger boat laden with full cargo for market, he was absolutely astounded at the boldness of such a deed. John entered the event in his diary:[56]

> On the night of the 18th of September, 1818, between the hours of 12 and ½ past 1, the wild Indians cut adrift from the wharf at Lower Sandy Point, Exploits, a boat loaded with salmon. The boat was found the next day, stranded on an island near Grego, or Gray Gull Island; sails gone and considerable other property stolen or destroyed. Guns, pistols, watch, money and many articles of personal apparel too numerous to mention. Cargo but little damaged.

A detailed account of this event as given by James Howley[57] was, he said "the story as I had it from the lips of the late John Peyton."

> While prosecuting the salmon fishery and fur trade in the bay and river of Exploits, he was much tormented by the depredations of the Indians, who came, usually in the night time, and pilfered everything they could lay hands upon. The articles stolen were not often of great value, and consisted generally of such things as knives, axes, traps, hooks, lines, rope and canvas. Annoying as this undoubtedly was, Mr. Peyton bore with it for a long time, and without using any retaliative measures. At length

the Indians became so emboldened as to commit a theft and act of destruction of more than ordinary character, which he could not overlook. Mr. Peyton was living at the time at Lower Sandy Point, in the Bay of Exploits, his house and stores stood upon the sloping bank of the river and a long wharf, built on piers, extended from the shore out to the deep water. On this occasion, his large open boat, loaded with the season's produce, lay at the head of the wharf, ready to proceed down the bay to market. It was one of those old style of boats, open amidship, with a cuddy at the forward and after ends, somewhat on the line of the ancient caravel. Besides the cargo of salmon and furs, Mr. Peyton had stowed away in the cuddies his clothes, bedding and several articles of value, including two silver watches, and some coins which were in his vest pockets, and there were also two guns and ammunition, culinary and other utensils aboard for use on the voyage.

Everything being in readiness, he and his crew were awaiting daylight and the turn of the tide to proceed on their journey. The night was very dark, and knowing that the Indians were about, a strict watch was kept, but seeing no prospect for a favourable time up till past midnight, he directed his men to lie down and take a rest while he himself would remain on guard. He took frequent turns up and down the wharf, and at one time said he thought he descried a dark object lying on the beach not far off which he was about to investigate, when one of his men assured him it was a splitting table that had been left there during the day, so he did not pay further heed to it. As the night drew on and everything appeared quiet, he concluded nothing would be disturbed during the few remaining hours before dawn, so feeling somewhat tired himself, he took one more thorough survey and then retired to the house to rest for a while. He threw himself down on a couch without removing his clothing, but he was so restless and uneasy that he could not sleep. An hour or so may have elapsed, when he jumped up again and visited the wharf. To his great mortification he found the boat with all its effects gone, and in the inky darkness could find no clue to the direction taken by the marauders.

He now called all his crew, and as soon as daylight made its appearance, started in pursuit. After many hours search they at length found the boat hauled up in a small creek at the mouth of Charles Brook, away down on the other side of the bay. She was completely rifled, everything of a portable nature, including the cordage and sails being carried off. The guns alone, battered and broken, and otherwise rendered perfectly useless, were found in the bed of the brook not far away. To follow up the trail just then would be very difficult and most probably futile.

The winters of 1815, 1816 and 1817 were ones of desolation and hunger amongst the settlers of the new colony. The population was increasing in large numbers with the influx of Irish emigrants. Inadequate supplies of imported provisions were due to the poor credit standings of the local merchants at the time. Any local endeavours, such as those of the Peyton entrepreneurs, were looked upon as welcome sources of employment.

The Peyton men could not tolerate any more disruptions in their business. Their loss of property in the recent incident totalled approximately £190 sterling. The articles stolen or destroyed by the Beothuk were very difficult to replace, as many items would have to be brought in by ship from England. The damage done to the boat required extensive repairs. The Peyton business venture had been successful despite such adversities. The father and son wished to see its success continue, not only for their own survival, but for the sake of their apprentices and employees.

Twenty-five-year-old John, who had been made a Conservator of the Peace, wished for complaints on this matter to go through the proper channels.

He became the spokesman for himself and his father and proceeded to St. John's to lay his complaint before the government authorities. His objective was "to endeavour to be on

good terms with Indians for the protection of my property."
Also he believed in "the rescuing of that tribe of our fellow
creatures from the misery and persecution they are exposed
to..."[58]

The government authorities at first were reluctant to
believe that such thievery by the Beothuk had taken place.
However, Sir Charles Hamilton "gave a full credence to it."[59] As
Governor he authorized John to try and retrieve his stolen
property which was vital to his work and to the men in his
employ. John was empowered by the governor to capture, if
possible, one or more of the native Beothuk Indians, alive, in
order to establish a friendly relationship through communication with the others in the tribe.[60]

John returned to the Bay of Exploits to his work and to
make plans. The late autumn of that year, 1818, did not appear
to be the appropriate time of year to pursue the suspected cul-
prits. He decided it would be better to wait until the winter to
undertake such a journey, when the tribe would be gathered
together in their winter encampments.

He was now familiar with Beothuk customs and their habitat. He suspected they would be encamped well into the interi-
or of the island, around the area now known as Red Indian
Lake. This lengthy journey had to be undertaken on foot so it
was imperative to go at the appropriate time of year.

The month of March 1819 was chosen for the expedition;
the rivers and ponds would be frozen solid, and generally the
heaviest snowfalls would be over. By then the days would be
lengthening, the sun's rays softening and settling the snow in

the daytime, followed by frosty nights, ideal conditions for early morning travelling. This was essential for the sledges of provisions that had to be hauled along the journey.

John set his course along the frozen Exploits River, the area he knew so well, to where he thought the winter head-quarters of the Beothuks might be. Along with his elderly father, he and several of the hardiest trappers, employees of Miller and Peyton Sr., prepared for the lengthy and difficult journey. Thomas Peyton wrote: "This was at [my father's] own expense. I do not know the exact number of men but should say eight to ten. I was acquainted with four of them."

John included his father in the expedition since he was a skilled and hardy woodsman with experience from similar previous treks. It seems now an unwise decision for John to have included his elderly father. At seventy-two years, an inveterate enemy of the Beothuk, the older Peyton was well known and disliked by them. His presence alone was sufficient to cause mistrust of the motives of these white men. It was in defence of this elderly man that the Peyton expedition became a tragedy, for unfortunately Beothuk blood was shed.

7

The Capture of Demasduit (Mary March)

March 1, 1819 dawned with good weather for the planned expedition into the interior. The Peyton men were anxious to accomplish the task of recovering, if possible, their possessions from the Beothuks and "to take some of the Indians and thus through them open a friendly communication with the rest."[61]

In preparation for the journey, the men of the party congregated at Upper Sandy Point, where they joined John and his father, and from there began the long trek. The cold weather made it possible to travel on the frozen Exploits River as they had planned.

Besides John and his father, the group consisted of eight of Miller and Peyton Sr.'s hardiest and most experienced trappers who were used to privations and the fatigue of woods travel. They were Richard "Dick" Richmond, John Day, "Jacky Jones" Snelgrove, Butler, Carey and three others. It is believed that the three were Thomas Taylor, Matthew Hughster and William Cull. They were amongst the oldest of the firm and had been on a similar expedition eight years earlier with Captain David Buchan and the marines of HMS *Adonis* in 1810–1811. Captain Buchan was quoted as saying at the time, "Taylor was well acquainted with this part of the country."[62]

During the Buchan expedition, Taylor had warned Buchan of the dangers of leaving two of his marines alone with the Beothuks while the rest of the crew returned to the ship for provisions. Buchan apparently did not heed Taylor's advice and these two marines, Corporal James Butler and Private Thomas Bouthland, were later found beheaded, stripped of clothing and with arrows piercing their backs.[63]

The Journal of Thomas Peyton, J.P., states:

> Thomas Taylor, a servant of my grandfather [John Peyton the elder], then residing at the Exploits River was the principal guide to this expedition [with Captain Buchan 1810–11]. He described the whole as a great blunder on the part of Buchan. Having resided for so many years previous, he [Taylor] was pretty well acquainted with the tactics of the aborigines and warned Capt. Buchan of what may [sic] happen; telling him plainly that on leaving the men that they would never see them alive again, for which he [Taylor] received a severe reprimand.

Buchan's expedition ended in failure after this unfortunate incident.

The Peyton crew, in preparation for their journey, had to estimate carefully the quantities of staple and unperishable foodstuffs needed to last out a possible lengthy time in the wilderness. The diet generally consisted of salted pork, hard biscuits, rice, dried peas, raisins, tea and cocoa. Everything was stored in kegs and casks for easy transportation. The remainder of the diet was left to chance and to the luck of the hunter for whatever wild game was encountered en route, such as ptarmigan (partridge), ducks, geese, hares or perhaps even deer.

At night the men had to kindle fires, around which they slept. These bivouacs were fenced around with boughs to shield them from piercing winds and provide a measure of warmth. Large boughs placed upside down in layers on the snow became the foundations for their beds.

There was frostbite to contend with and every precaution had to be taken to guard against it. The severity of the cold winds coupled with low temperatures often caused "frost burn," extreme cases when the flesh, benumbed with cold, was rendered without feeling. The extremities, fingers, toes and often the whole of the feet, were especially prone. As a preventative measure to protect the face, the men wore "pinovers": pieces of wool flannel attached to the cap to pin over the nose and chin and another piece to protect the nape of the neck.

Another affliction to guard against was "snow blindness." During the sunny March days, the expanse of white snow made dazzling by the reflection of the sun's rays, caused severe spasms of the eyelids, causing painful tears and distress to the eyes to the point of blindness. The days of the journey were recorded:[64]

DAY 1, MARCH 1, 1819:
All ten men started out on foot, carrying snowshoes and hauling sleds of provisions.

DAY 2, MARCH 2, 1819:
A few Beothuk wigwams were sighted along the way but no Indians. These wigwams were not presently in use but believed

to have been used by the natives in the spring and autumn for deer hunting.

DAY 3, MARCH 3, 1819:
Spotted a fireplace by the side of a brook where it appeared Indians may have camped a few days previously.

DAY 4, MARCH 4, 1819:
Came upon a storehouse used by the Indians to store caribou meat. Five "marten cat" traps, stolen from the furriers, were found inside; also found a part of the canvas jib of the wrecked caravel. Tracks in the snow suggested that the Indians had moved in a southwest direction only the day previously. Travelled until dark. Weather intensely cold.

The majority of the crew's provisions were left at this storehouse site, in order to speed up the pursuit. Having travelled a considerable distance in four days, John Jr. now felt he was coming closer to the Indian's trail and he felt he would soon be nearing their winter encampment. The men continued their difficult trek until nightfall when they set up camp.

Although the weather was extremely cold, no fire was permitted that night lest the smoke give away their position. John Jr. did not wish to alarm the Indians by appearing to be on the attack, but he hoped to get close to them and appease and show them that no harm was intended.

DAY 5, MARCH 5, 1819:
This was an eventful day. It dawned a frosty winter morning. Strong winds and the heavy drifting of snow added to the severity of the cold temperatures. After a cold and uncomfortable night and cold food, the men commenced walking at daybreak.

On the fifth day, the party having traversed several more miles, they came to an area generally known as "the great pond," sometimes referred to as Lieutenant's Lake or Lake Bathurst (now Red Indian Lake). Fresh tracks were seen in the snow. Following the direction of the footprints, in the early afternoon the men came upon a small band of Beothuks encamped near the shores of the frozen lake.

A lone Indian seemed unable to keep up with the others as they scattered into the nearby woods from the wigwams. This lone Indian became a target for pursuit.

On seeing the Englishmen, the native ran screaming towards the woods in the direction of the others who had fled. Young John Peyton, in the full strength of his youth, quickly shed his heavy jacket and snowshoes, enabling him to gain on the native. The Indian appeared frightened as John neared and kept glancing back at him. John dropped the gun he was carrying onto the snow, pointing to it and holding up his arms; his gesture intended to show he meant no harm. The Indian stopped.

John was unable to tell whether the native was male or female, but the question was soon resolved, for the Indian opened her deerskin cassock at the neck, revealing her breasts, in an appeal to John for mercy. He walked up to her and held out his hand, as a sign of friendship. She placed her hand in his and then the men in the Peyton party came towards the pair.

Other members of her tribe then appeared. Two of them tried to force John into letting the woman go; another was carrying a concealed hatchet under his deerskin tunic, but had it quickly taken from him by John's men.

A very tall Indian suddenly noticed the elder Peyton. He recognized him as their enemy from previous encounters and thinking him to be the "ringleader," must have thought that there was now a chance to wreak his revenge.

The elderly Peyton was attacked by the Indian, who tried to grasp the old man's gun. Unsuccessful, the Indian then grabbed the old man by the throat and in the skirmish they moved about fifty yards from the others. The elder Peyton appeared to be in imminent danger.

It was only natural that John would attempt to protect his elderly father. He ordered his men to strike the attacker to release his grasp on the elder Peyton's throat. His father was free for the moment.

Meanwhile several more Indians advanced against the group of Englishmen. The elderly Peyton was again attacked. He was shaken so violently by the tall Indian that he yelled for help. According to John Day, one of the party, the elder Peyton shouted out, "Are you going to stand by and let the Indian kill me?"[65]

Again the Indian attacked the white man by the throat, more strongly than before. The other Englishmen saw the dangerous predicament the older man was in. John Day, who had been a servant of Peyton Sr., yelled, "Do you think master's life is in danger?" to which the others answered, "Yes."[66] The Indian hung grimly on. According to John Day later, Peyton would soon have been choked to death.

In the utter confusion of natives rushing amongst the crew, the younger Peyton, to save his father's life, again ordered his men to defend him. Shots were fired and the Indian attacking the elderly man was killed. It all happened so quickly that the younger John, in his testimony later, said that the shots were fired so close together that he could not distinguish how many were fired, for they appeared as a single shot.

It has not been recorded what orders were given to the men or if in fact any orders were given at all by John, with the exception of the order to protect his father. Neither is it known for certain which man or men shot the Beothuk attacker. There is no documented proof. John's policy was always to avoid violence. However, at the time of his father's attack, he was a considerable distance away, with the captured Beothuk native in his hand, apparently his gun already thrown aside. He did not seem to be in a position to go to his father's defence.

According to James Hailey,[67] Thomas Peyton had said, "[Richmond] was an old brute. He was one of my father's party at the capture of Mary March. He it was who shot her husband at that time and caused all the trouble."

The unfortunate victim lay sprawled on the snow. The remainder of the tribe, frightened, fled under cover of the thick forest. The slain Indian, who later was found to be the Beothuk chief, was also supposedly the mate of the captured woman.

If his main intent had been to rescue his mate, why didn't he attack the younger John, who was holding her captive? Apparently he was more intent on seeking revenge on the older Peyton for his mistreatment of the natives in previous years.

One of the men of the party, John Day, later told of how the Beothuk chief, when first advancing toward the Englishmen, "broke off a piece of fir bough, placing it on his forehead as a flag of truce,"[68] in hopes of rescuing the woman. Had more heed been paid and a less aggressive approach been made, allowing the chief and his mate to reunite, perhaps friendship and understanding could have been achieved. Hostility may have been avoided. But it was not to be. Neither group trusted the other.

The body of the slain Indian was covered with boughs by Peyton's men and a quick examination was made of the campsite. They found their stolen sails covering one of the wigwams, and their gear and sundry articles that had been taken from them. John's personal effects, the watches and coins, were strung on deerskin thongs to make necklaces and charms.

Thomas Peyton was later to write in his journal: "Everything was found in a confused state. Nothing was touched or taken away that I ever heard of unless it was some small article of no value."

While there, John collected some small object belonging to the Indians, as a souvenir of this extraordinary meeting with the natives. The tag he used to later mark the object read:

Taken from a Red Indian wigwam at Lake Bathurst [now Red Indian Lake] at the caption [capture] of a Red Indian woman on the 5th March 1819, afterward named or known as Mary March.
By John Peyton stipend Magistrate, Twillingate, Newfoundland, formerly of the Navy pay office, Somerset House, London. Presented to T.G.B Lloyde [sic] Esq., Geological Society, Somerset House, London. Aug. 17, 1875.[69]

This object could have been a primitive stone tool or stone arrowhead. Many years later one was presented to T.G.B. Lloyd when he came to Newfoundland and made a collection of Beothuk stone implements.[70] Lloyd later wrote three treatises on Beothuk culture for the Journal of the Anthropological Institute of Great Britain and Ireland.[71]

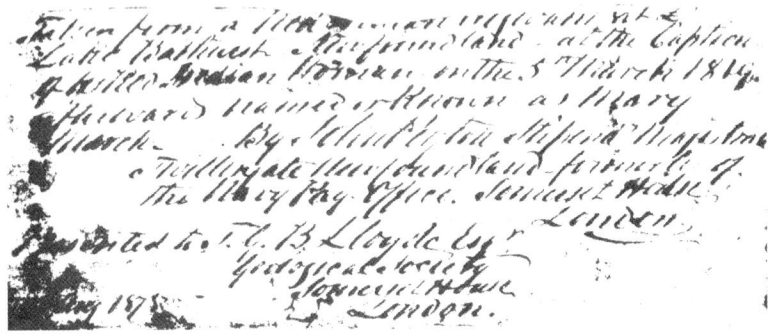

Tag used by John Peyton Jr. to denote a stone implement taken from a wigwam, March 5, 1819

As the Peyton party prepared to return home from the interior of the island, every consideration was given to their captive. She was young, about twenty-three or twenty-four years of age, of copper brown complexion, black hair and high cheek bones. She was found to be of gentle disposition. At the time of her capture she was wearing a tunic make of deerskin and trimmed with "marten cat" fur. On her feet she wore crude moccasins, also made of deerskin.

It took several days for the party to return from the interior to the coast. Throughout the journey the captured woman was drawn on a sled covered with blankets to protect her from the cold temperatures. She often wailed in grief, obviously for her husband and her people. During the nightly encampments she made several attempts to escape. She noiselessly crawled along the snow, dragging her blanket to obliterate her tracks. When she realized her attempts to escape were futile she kept close to John Jr. all the while, "as though for protection, no doubt recognizing him as the leader of the party and a man superior in every way to his fellows." To the man[72] who killed her husband she showed her dislike by never allowing him to come near her.

In order to communicate with her captors she acted out words in pantomime and made herself understood. It was learned that her name was Demasduit. She was soon dubbed Mary March by her captors, March being the month of her

capture. It was also learned that her slain mate's name was Nonosabasut.

After a lengthy and diffi-cult return journey the men of the expedition reached their dwellings on the Exploits River banks without further incident. John, unmarried, had no one to care for Mary March at his father's residence at

Beothuk native Mary March

Upper Sandy Point on the Exploits estuary. As a result, she was immediately taken to Twillingate and placed in Reverend Leigh's charge where she was tended by a Mrs. Cockburn. Reverend Leigh was the

Episcopal missionary there and also a Justice of the Peace. A decision had to be made by John and Reverend Leigh on the next procedure to follow. John, his task completed, left Mary March in Reverend Leigh's care and returned again to his home on the Exploits River and to his elderly father.

Mary March was never sheltered at Twillingate by John Peyton Jr., as has often been suggested. He was not living there at that time and didn't move to Twillingate to live until 1836.

Reverend Leigh hoped to learn the Beothuk language from Mary March while she was staying at his home, but when it became known that she had left a child behind, it was urgent that she be returned to her people. She gave them to understand that if she was reunited with her child she would return again to captivity.

A short time later, after the spring thaw and the opening of navigation, Reverend Leigh decided to take the Beothuk woman to St. John's to meet the governor and await further orders. He was accompanied on the voyage by the man who had captured her. Apparently John Peyton Jr. had hoped he could undertake a second expedition into the interior, using Mary March as a go-between, to establish communications and a friendly relationship with her tribe. In his letter of May 31, 1819 to Governor Hamilton offering his services, he wrote:[73]

> ...My object was and still is to endeavour to be on good terms with the Indians from the protection of my property, and the rescuing of that tribe of our fellow creatures from the misery and persecution they are exposed to in the interior from Micmacs, and on the exterior by the whites. With this impression on my mind I offer my services to the Government for the

ensuing summer and I implore Your Excellency to lend me any assistance you may think proper. I cannot afford to do much at my own expense, having nothing but what I work for, the expenses of doing anything during the summer would be less than the winter, as it will not be safe ever to attempt going into their country with so small a crew as I had with me last winter. Still these expenses are much greater than I can afford, as nothing effectual can be expected to be done under £400. Unless your excellency should prefer sending an expedition on the service out of the fleet, in which case I would leave the woman [Mary March] at Your Excellency's disposal, but should I be appointed to cruise the summer for them, and which I do not do and find me and necessaries under £400, I have not the least doubt but that I shall, through the medium of the woman I now have, be enabled to open an intercourse with them, nor is it all improbable but that she will return with us again if she can procure an infant she left behind her. I beg to assure Your Excellency from my acquaintance with the bays and the place of resort for the Indians during the summer, that I am most confident of succeeding in the plan here laid down. I have the honour to be, Your Excellency's very humble and obedient servant.

(signed) John Peyton Jr.

James P. Howley in his book *The Beothuks or Red Indians* wrote:

It's a pity Peyton's offer was not accepted, as he knew more about them and their ways than any other living person. With the aid of the woman it is probable he might have succeeded in opening communication with her tribe, of which he expresses himself so confident.

Four days later the Governor's decision was made known. His intentions were to dispatch the HMS *Sir Francis Drake*, in command of Captain W.N. Glascock, to proceed northward to Notre Dame Bay to endeavour to return the Indian woman to her tribe, to search out her child, and if possible open up communications with her countrymen. The governor also gave orders to procure the services of Reverend Leigh and young John Peyton to accompany the woman on the proposed trip.

In the meantime an investigation of her capture, and the circumstances of the shooting of the Beothuk chief was carried out. The men of the Peyton expedition were questioned and statements taken from each man. While at St. John's, the younger John, as leader of the party, was brought before the Grand Jury of Newfoundland and the matter thoroughly investigated. The following statement summed up the findings of the jury:[74]

> ...The Grand Jury are of the opinion that no malice preceded the transaction, and that there was no intention on the part of Peyton's party to get possession of any of them [the Indians] by such violence as would occasion bloodshed. It appears that the deceased came by his death in consequence of the attack on Peyton Sr., and his subsequent obstinacy, and not desisting when repeatedly menaced by some of the party for that purpose, and the peculiar situation of the Peytons and their men, was such as to warrant their acting on the defensive...

John, in his account of the matter, wrote:[75]

> ...Could we have intimidated or persuaded him [the Indian] to leave us, or even have seen the others go off, we should have been most happy to have spared using violence, but when it was remembered that our small party were in the heart of the Indian country, one hundred miles from any European settlement, and that there were in our sight at times as many Indians as our party amounted to, and we could not ascertain how many were in the woods that we did not see, it could not be avoided with safety to ourselves...

Governor Hamilton in his dispatch of September 1819, to
Earl Bathurst, the Colonial Secretary in England, wrote:[76]

> ..The circumstances of the transactions on the lake were by my
> desire laid before and minutely investigated by the Grand Jury,
> who were of the opinion that the party were fully justified under
> all circumstances in acting as they did, on the defensive. I men-
> tion this as a proof to Your Lordship that no wanton act of cru-
> elty was committed or attempted by Mr. Peyton or his men...

Many interpretations over the years of this incident of
March 5, 1819, have laid a great shadow on the younger John
Peyton. Although history has not been kind, it is a more seri-
ous charge that it has not been accurate.

8

Exploring with Captain W.N. Glascock

T he younger John's integrity and knowledge were very much valued in that same year of 1819 by Captain William Nugent Glascock of HMS *Sir Francis Drake* and Captain David Buchan of HMS *Grasshopper*. John's services as pilot and guide to both men were highly commended by both captains. Thomas Peyton noted in his journal: "In the summer of 1819, my father was engaged in piloting HMS brig *Drake* in making a survey of the bay and river Exploits, Captain Glascock commander."

Meanwhile the Beothuk woman Mary March had been sent back from St. John's to Twillingate by Governor Hamilton, again in Reverend Leigh's care. While at St. John's she contracted a heavy cold and appeared to be generally in a poor state of health. She was to remain at Twillingate while awaiting the ship *Drake* whose captain had received orders to return her, if possible, to her people, to search for her child and to open up communication with her tribe.

The *Drake*, sailing out of St. John's, was a supply ship for the two survey vessels *Scrub Tender* and *Sydney*, then surveying

Bonavista Bay. After unloading supplies to these two ships en route, the captain's further orders were to proceed to Morton's Harbour on New World Island; the ship was to be a headquarters for the exploration and search of Exploits and Notre Dame bays. Here the ship was to await the arrival of the younger John Peyton from the Exploits River, and Reverend Leigh with the Beothuk woman from Twillingate.

The Bay of Notre Dame had not yet been surveyed. John's navigational knowledge of the area was useful in piloting the *Drake* and under his direction, the smaller boats, shallops and gigs, were also to undertake the voyage throughout the inlets of the bay and on into the mouth of the Exploits River in search of Mary March's people.

After the *Drake*'s arrival at Morton's Harbour it was soon found that the harbour was too great a distance from any desirable entry point into Indian territory. After completing some survey work of the area and repairs made to the sloop, the *Drake* sailed directly across the mouth of Notre Dame Bay to Fortune Harbour, where she lay at anchor. It appeared a simpler task on that side of the bay, in more sheltered waters, for the sloop's gig (a small boat manned by several sets of oars) and cutter (a single-masted, gaff-rigged sailing boat) to cruise the Indian territory of New Bay, the Charles Brook area, Exploits Bay and the Exploits River, areas that John knew well.

Before leaving St. John's, the governor had delivered to Captain Glascock many gifts and trinkets that were thought to be of use and interest to the Indians. They included blankets, red frocks and cloaks, red shirts, strings of beads, looking

glasses [mirrors], tin cooking utensils, hatchets, knives, fishing
gear and many other sundries.

In his orders to Captain Glascock, Governor Hamilton
wrote:[77]

> ...the coast on which you are likely to find these Indians has
> never been surveyed, and is little known, but is represented as
> being very dangerous. You will leave His Majesty's Sloop at
> Morton's Harbour and proceed with your boats, entering such
> bays and rivers as may be most likely to be frequented by the
> Indians during the summer season. But this is not to prevent
> your proceeding in the *Drake* to some other port further to the
> northward, if you can without unnecessary risk or hazard effect
> it with the assistance of any person acquainted with the coast.
> As the principal objects in view are to return the female Indian
> in question to her tribe and to establish a friendly communica-
> tion with these aborigines, great care must be taken to select for
> this enterprise such persons of the crew as are most orderly
> and obedient, and every proper means you can suggest used to
> bring them to an interview, in doing which, as the greater cau-
> tion must be observed, it will be advisable to refrain from using
> firearms for any purpose before these objectives are accom-
> plished.
>
> Notwithstanding these instructions, the best mode of
> returning this female Indian to her friends, and of effecting an
> amicable intercourse with them, must in a great degree depend
> upon local and unforseen circumstances.
>
> It is therefore entirely left to your own discretion in con-
> junction with the Reverend Mr. Leigh, under the fullest reliance
> upon your care and attention to her while she is under your
> protection, but it would be advisable that you should take that
> gentleman and Mr. Peyton Jr., with you in the boats, and none
> others except those who may be absolutely serviceable on such
> an expedition.

Captain Glascock's exploration days record:[78]

JUNE 3, 1819:
Received orders to sail from St. John's.

JUNE 17, 1819:
With John Peyton Jr. and Mary March on board, the *Drake* sailed for Fortune Harbour, where the vessel moored at anchor, to be used as a headquarters for the cruises in and around the bay.

JUNE 18, 1819:
Captain Glascock with a small crew, John Peyton, and Mary March proceeded by cutter and gig to New Bay, a place known to have often been frequented by the Beothuks but they failed to see any. Returned to the sloop *Drake* two days later without even seeing any trace of the natives.

JUNE 22, 1819:
Captain Glascock with a small crew, John and Mary March left by cutter and cruised through the Bay of Exploits and on into the Exploits River. Having reached the first falls [later named the Bishop's Falls] by nightfall, rowing was done with muffled oars, so as not to be detected by the natives.

JUNE 24, 1819:
Captain Glascock and John entered the woods on the banks of the Exploits River in search of wigwams. The only ones seen were those vacated by the natives the previous winter.

JUNE 25, 1819:
Captain Glascock and party still unsuccessful so far in their endeavours to meet with any of the natives. Returned again with Mary March to their headquarters aboard the *Drake* at Fortune Harbour.

The Indian woman did not appear to be in a very robust condition for travelling daily in open boats. Her heavy cold had apparently turned to consumption, although this was unknown to anyone at that time. The disease had been prevalent amongst the whites and she, apparently in a delicate state of health, was highly susceptible. Due to her poor health she was allowed to rest for the next few days aboard the *Drake*.

During this time Captain Glascock assigned John Trivick as navigator to cruise in the cutter to the Badger Bay area for several days to survey and sketch the extent of the area in preparation for yet another search for the natives.

JUNE 28, 1819:
On being told that the natives had returned again to the Exploits River banks, Captain Glascock with a small crew and John Peyton checked this out; the crew again using muffled oars after nightfall. This trip proved uneventful. The mosquitoes and black flies were an ordeal. After two more days of cruising southward to Indian Arm the party returned to the sloop. Captain Glascock and three of his crew became ill, their eyelids so badly swollen from the mosquito bites, as to cause temporary blindness.

JUNE 30, 1819:
John Trivick and crew while on assignment in Badger Bay spotted three Beothuks crossing Flat Rock Tickel [sic]. In an unfortunate episode of Trivick discharging his musket to confuse the natives, they were lost sight of. He entered the incident in his log.

Trivick was later requested by the governor to make a statement regarding the matter. He wrote:[79]

...Acknowledge the receipt of your letter... requiring me to state what took place when I fell in with a party of native Indians in a canoe about 150 yards distance, and 50 from the shore. I immediately made towards them endeavouring to make them understand that we wished to communicate with them, but they showed no disposition to listen to us, were evidently getting away, and might if they got ashore easily escape into the woods, where it would be fruitless to follow them; under these circumstances I thought the only means left me to come up with them, was by firing a musket and thus throwing them into confusion, which it partially effected, but being by this time near the shore they unfortunately escaped as I anticipated.

I beg further to state that the almost certain hope of being able to intercept them before they got on shore, together with my anxiety and the utter impossibility of tracing them through the woods, could possibly have induced me so far to deviate from Capt. Glascock's orders [not] to fire...

Governor Hamilton in his Colonial report to Earl Bathurst stated:[80]

An officer of HMS sloop *Drake* has used firearms during an attempt to fall in with some of the Indians in their summer haunts. This was a direct violation of orders. Believed he acted through an error in judgment.

Thomas Peyton when later writing of the incident said:

I suppose the distance across the tickel [sic] at this point would be thirty chains, more or less. I heard my father say that they certainly would have caught up only the officer in charge of the boat stopped the men from rowing in order to get the Arms Chest out. He told me he was very vexed at the officer to think, as he said, of a boat's crew commanded by a British officer, not being able to do this without weapons.

JULY 1, 1819:
John Trivick having sighted Beothuks the day previously in Badger Bay, a gig, with a small crew and John Peyton, under the *Drake's* Lieutenant were dispatched to the area.

JULY 5, 1819
Captain Glascock now feeling up to duty, left by cutter with Mary March to join the other two boats in the same area of Badger Bay. The first day out, towards evening Beothuks were sighted in a canoe. On reaching the spot where they were seen to land, the Glascock party also landed and searched the area. Mary March remained aboard the cutter and according to Glascock "exhibiting an apathetic indifference" as to the fate of her countrymen. Captain Glascock on his return to the cutter gave Mary March the option of following the members of her

tribe into the woods for the purpose of joining them or staying with her captors. She made the choice to stay. No doubt her listless apathy was indicative of her advancing consumptive condition for she showed no desire to go ashore.

JULY 6, 1819:
It was intended for the crews to land at the same place as before, where the Indians were seen to land the day previously. On examining the situation it was decided against this, withdrawing the three boats lest the Indians suspect it to be an attack. Instead, under John's direction, the Indian paths throughout a stretch of over thirty miles of coastline, were followed in search of wigwams. Only old ones, unoccupied, were found.

JULY 9, 1819:
In a final attempt to meet up with some of the natives, Lieutenant Munbee, accompanied by John and Mary March, proceeded in another direction, once more to Badger Bay and Seal Bay. This time they were guided through Indian paths by Mary March to some wigwams, again found to be unoccupied. Presents were left in these wigwams to show the natives of intended friendliness. After four days of travelling the crew returned with the captive to the sloop. She could not be prevailed upon to remain behind.

JULY 14, 1819:
Captain Glascock decided to call off the expedition and return his ship *Sir Francis Drake* back to St. John's.

He had covered ninety miles of coastline with his crew and many more miles on foot inland in a continuous search of the natives over a period of twenty-six days, without success. His ship was running short of food supplies and his men had endured many privations, the loss of necessary sleep and comforts, although showing great fortitude. He wrote,"The most zealous and active energy manifested by the officers and ship's company I ever witnessed. They have suffered much in consequence of being exposed

of upwards of a week at a time in open boats, but custom would
have seasoned them to this, could they have taken their natural rest
by sleep, of which they were totally deprived by the tormenting
tortures of every description of insects which infest this coast."[81]

Captain Glascock in his report of John Peyton wrote:

> I cannot, Sir, conclude this detail without mentioning to you the
> steady, zealous and ever active conduct of Mr. Peyton, Jr., whose
> exertions were unexampled to accomplish the desired purpose
> for which he accompanied me. His whole time has been devot-
> ed to this service, and I don't hesitate to pronounce it to be my
> opinion that Your Excellency could not have selected a more
> proper person to assist me in the execution of your orders.[82]

The Indian woman, Mary March, was again, for a third
time, taken back to Twillingate, and once more placed in
Reverend Leigh's care. John then returned to his home, supervising his salmon stations and continuing his judicial duties.
Six days later the *Drake* arrived at St. John's. The expedition
had not been successful.

Usually Midshipman Sidney Smith of the *Drake* was
assigned as crew member of the cutter or gig to which John
was assigned as pilot. They became friends. Smith too was
impressed by the grandeur of the Exploits River and also took
interest in the Newfoundland breed of dogs. Before 1770 it was
known as "the Bear dog" and kept by John as a work dog.
Horses had not yet been introduced to parts of Notre Dame
Bay so the Newfoundland dog then took their place, hauling
firewood, dried codfish and shipbuilding materials.

After Midshipman Smith left the Exploits area to return to
St. John's in the *Drake* in July 1819, the younger John's

Newfoundland bitch produced a litter. When the puppies were a few weeks old, John sent two to St. John's, one for Midshipman Smith of the *Drake* and one for Chief Justice Forbes. There is a letter sent to John thirty-one years later via a schooner's captain from England, before Newfoundland had inaugurated a postal service.

The letter was sent by former Midshipman Smith, by this time Captain Sidney Smith. It reads:[83]

TO: JOHN PEYTON   TILMANSTONE
RIVER EXPLOITS   NEAR SANDWICH, KENT
                                                               OCT. 18, 1850

Dear Sir,

Being casually at Poole and receiving an offer from Capt. Cheeseman to convey this letter, I take the liberty to surprise you. We were acquainted during a few weeks, rather more than 31 years ago! But as I have never forgotten you, so you cannot have forgotten me.

I was midshipman in the boats of His Majesty's Brig *Drake*, Capt. Glascock, some short time employed in exploring the River Exploits, under your pilotage, with your Red Indian captive, in 1819. I went up the river as far as it was navigable for a canoe, was much charmed with the scenery, with your friendship and kindness, and with your romantic way of life.

You sent after me to St. John's a puppy of your breed (in conjunction with one for Chief Justice Forbes.) My dog was eventually carried by my father to Caen in Normandy where they both died of old age, the dog first. His body was begged by the public museum as the finest specimen of his variety the French had ever seen. He was stuffed and is at this moment a conspicuous ornament in the gallery of Natural History, Hotel de Ville, Caen.

I have no time to add more than express my satisfaction to learn from Capt. Cheeseman that you are alive and well.

Your obliged servant,
W. Sidney Smith, Capt. R.N.

The notes of Thomas Peyton (circa 1906) say:

The *Drake* was afterwards lost on the west coast of Newfoundland. Captain Baker was then in command and was drowned while endeavouring to save his ship's company.

In those same notes he wrote:

Badger Bay and Seal Bay used to be much frequented by the Indians; being an ideal place for birds, young seals, also for salmon and trout. At the brooks in the bottom of those bays there are now pools or round holes [formed by the natural action of water spinning in tiny whirlpools] worked in the rock (Soap Stone) where the Indians used to put seal fat. These spots are open to the sun and young seal fat would render out in them very quickly.

9

Journey with Captain David Buchan

A lthough Captain Glascock's summer expedition did not prove successful, Governor Hamilton still wished a further search to be conducted of the same area, in hope of establishing contact with Mary March's people.

Captain David Buchan of HMS *Grasshopper* was commissioned on August 8, 1819 to carry out the expedition. He had visited the same area in 1810–11 while a Lieutenant on HMS *Adonis.*

Peyton's expedition earlier in the year had proved to be more successful during the winter months, prompting Captain Buchan to undertake this second expedition after the winter season had begun. John Peyton was to act as guide. Buchan set sail from St. John's on September 25, 1819 with the following instructions:[84]

...Whereas the establishment of an amicable intercourse with the native Indians of this island is an object to which my attention is particularly directed by His Majesty's instructions, and is highly to be desired as affording future means of extending to that miserable people the blessing of civilization. And whereas I have great confidence that from your known zeal, prudence and perseverance joined to the advantages arising from the previous local knowledge gained by you on a former expedition of the same nature, the best hopes may be entertained of a successful result to an enterprise of so much interest. You are therefore hereby required and directed to complete the provisions of His Majesty's Sloop for the winter... You will also be provided with such articles as are considered of use and interest to the native Indians, of which you will dispose of in such manner as you may deem best calculated to answer the intention... proceed in quest of the native Indians with the object already promised, of returning to her people the Indian woman before-mentioned and endeavouring by the best means in your power to open and establish a friendly intercourse with them...

When Captain Buchan arrived at Exploits Bay he took the *Grasshopper* into Peter's Arm, as far into the Exploits River mouth as possible, where she lay at anchor to serve as base for the journey up the Exploits River. In 1810–11 he had noted in his journal of the "great waterfall" (now Bishop's Falls); "The sound of this waterfall was at times plainly heard on board the schooner at Peter's Arm, from which [the falls] ascended a vapour that darkened the atmosphere for a considerable extent."

Here at Peter's Arm the crew of the *Grasshopper* made preparations for the long winter months ahead, the "freeze-up" when all navigation would cease and their vessel would be "frozen in," in its winter anchorage, not too far from John's shipyard at Indian Point on the south bank of the river estuary.

To last out a long stay at Peter's Arm, extra food supplies had to be brought from St. John's, before "freeze-up," to the site. John, as owner and master of the schooner *Susan,* was authorized to perform this duty. On an invoice totalling

approximately £30 and signed for by the ship's officer, S.H.
Hithom, Purser of HMS *Grasshopper* the list reads:[85]

> Invoice of provisions and victualling stores delivered on board
> the *Susan*, Schooner; John Peyton, Master, Sept. 16 and 17, 1819:
>
> Bread ....One hundred and thirty bags [hardtack]
> Beef ....Eight casks [pickled]
> Pork ....Seven casks [pickled]
> Suet ....Two casks [rendered lard]
> Raisins ....Two casks
> Sugar ....Three casks
> Cocoa ....Two casks
> Peas ....Five casks
> Spirits ....Ten casks
> Vinegar ....One cask
> Tobacco ....One very large Hogshead
> [usually 100- to 140-gallon size]

As for Mary March, Buchan was instructed through a letter to be delivered to Reverend Leigh, "...and that you will
therefore after consultation with him [Reverend Leigh] take
such measure for affecting the purpose [returning Mary March
to Captain Buchan's charge] as in your judgment may appear to
be most likely to lead a favourable result; but as those measures
must almost wholly depend upon local circumstances and con-
siderations, it is entirely left to your discretion to adopt such
course of proceeding as the information you will obtain may
suggest..."[86]

Again John was authorized to carry out another task; to
transport Mary March to the *Grasshopper* after she was
released from Reverend Leigh's care at Twillingate. They
arrived by schooner at Peter Arm on November 25, 1819 where

Mary March was put on board the *Grasshopper* with a woman companion to look after her.

John also boarded the ship for the duration, it being the headquarters for the planned expedition. Although John had been her captor, the Indian woman felt secure in his presence. Buchan wrote that Mary March "seemed always much satisfied when he was near and looked up to him as her protector."[87] Buchan immediately noticed the deterioration in her health since he had last seen her during the summer. He felt it was urgent to start the journey as soon as weather conditions permitted. He hoped to bring Mary March's people to her if possible, rather than have her travel to them. Her health did not appear strong enough for lengthy winter travel. Her main wish was to be united with her child.

As time dragged on through the late fall while final preparations were being carried out, the Beothuk woman's health steadily declined. As her strength lessened she often expressed to John and Captain Buchan her desire to accompany them in search of her child. She always appeared hopeful and cheerful that this trip would take place and they would be united.

John, who loved the outdoors, always took a daily walk. He enjoyed winter jaunts and tramping through the heavy January snowfalls. On January 8, while John was gone as usual for his morning's walk, Mary March was seized with a period of difficult breathing due to her consumptive state. After a short period she fully recovered. About fifteen minutes later she was again seized with difficulty breathing, almost to a point of suffocation. Captain Buchan and John were both sent for, but John had not returned from his walk. While in the presence of Captain Buchan, Mary March died. Captain Buchan reported to the governor: "Her last wish appears to have been to see Mr. Peyton, and she ceased to respire with his name upon her lips."[88]

When John returned to the *Grasshopper* he was very disturbed at this unfortunate turn of events. The captain and crew had not anticipated such a sad ending to the affair. Captain Buchan commented: "Her mild and gentle manners and great patience under much suffering endeared her to all, and her dissolution was deeply lamented by us."[89]

Immediately a change of plans had to be made by Captain Buchan; to return the corpse of Mary March to her tribe, with gifts, to eliminate any possibility of hostile feelings with the natives. Weather and ice conditions delayed any chance to continue until two weeks later, on January 21, when the party set out on the arduous journey on foot to convey Mary March's body up the Exploits River.

Since this expedition was to the same general area and during the wintertime as the Peyton expedition the year previously, similar preparations were made. Snowshoes had to be worn or carried. Muskets also had to be carried; provisions and conditions were such that the hunting of game was a necessity along the way. Sledges of unperishable food supplies had to be hauled along by the men. Precautions had to be taken to avoid frostbite and snow blindness.

Fires were kindled nightly around which the men took turns sleeping. Before the men could take their rest, boughs were cut at each campsite, for firewood, for bed foundations and as a wind barrier around the bivouac. Clothing was dried each night for the next day's travel, to avert frostbite. The seamen were unaccustomed to the severity of such winter weather and lengthy outdoor day- and night exposure. Their rations of spirits and tobacco were comforting morale boosters that helped keep the men going on their long and difficult trek.

The start of the journey was recorded as follows:[90]

DAY 1, JANUARY 21, 1820:
Captain Buchan, along with fifty of his crew members, and Peyton Jr. set out for the vicinity of Red Indian Lake. Also included was an auxiliary party of ten men along with a ship's officer, as an additional reinforcement for the first and most difficult part of the journey. The auxiliary party, engaged to prepare the way, were men familiar with the area, seasoned woodsmen of the Peyton firm. Sleds of staple provisions, necessary to last approximately for forty days, were hauled along by the men. One of the sleds bore a red coffin containing the body of Mary March.

DAY 6, JANUARY 26:
Several days of travel brought the party to the Indian paths. The going was found to be extremely rough and the ice conditions of the Exploits River were very treacherous. The sledges, not sufficiently strong enough to withstand so much hardship, became badly damaged. It took two days to repair them before proceeding.

DAY 7, JANUARY 27:
Due to former experience Captain Buchan felt that the most difficult part of the journey had been accomplished. It was decided by him to return the auxiliary party, plus one man suffering from frostbitten feet, back to their original habitats.

DAY 8, JANUARY 28:
The rafting of the ice, raised several feet high in some areas of the river forced an overflow of water over the ice surface. Great care

had to be taken to prevent the food supplies from becoming water damaged. Many of the men became wet and encountered great difficulty in averting frostbite due to severe cold weather.

DAYS 9, 10 AND 11, JANUARY 29, 30 AND 31:
Journeyed to just below Badger Bay Ponds where a bivouac was set up on the south side of the river. Midshipman Waller and John [Peyton] were sent on a reconnaissance so that the party could continue its journey in the morning. The two men crossed over to the other side of the river; John ascending a large tree to obtain a more commanding view of the area ahead. Meanwhile the ice of the swollen river became so violently agitated, the ice rafting and breaking loose with great swiftness, left John and the marine at great risk in rejoining the party. Later in the day the pent up river and the accumulation of the ice gave way in thunderous convulsions causing an overflow of water into the area of the bivouac. Only swift action on the part of the men saved the sledges of provisions and the remains of Mary March from utter destruction.

DAY 12, FEBRUARY 1:
Time was spent repairing the sledges and making things in readiness to again move on. Three of the seamen became lame, two of them from frostbitten feet and the other had accidentally chopped his foot with an axe.

DAY 13, FEBRUARY 2:
After a hazardous journey of twelve days with encounters of almost unsurmountable proportions amongst so many men, Captain Buchan found it necessary to send some men back to the *Grasshopper*, thirteen seamen accompanied by a midshipman. "The party was too cumbersome and there was great difficulty of getting the seamen to walk over the snow on rackets [snowshoes]. They were sent back to the ship while the remainder continued to proceed."

DAYS 14, 15, 16 AND 17:
Even after continuous repairs to the sledges, now only four out of twelve were still useable. Each individual man had to back pack a load of provisions for his own survival. Some evidence of Indians was sighted.

DAY 18, FEBRUARY 7:
The previous three days of heavy frost made travelling somewhat easier. The north bank of the river, the area in which they
were travelling, had been burned in a forest fire. It offered little
protection for an overnight camp. This made another dangerous
crossing of the river necessary in order to set up camp. The
river ice appeared so precarious as to restrict the men to cross
in single file for a mile and a half with whatever provisions each
man was capable of carrying.

DAY 19, FEBRUARY 8:
A return to the forest paths on the north bank necessitated a
treacherous re-crossing of the precarious river ice. It was not
long before the party came upon a winter hunting ground of the
Indians. Here were unoccupied wigwams, deer skins and stored
venison. Evidence clearly showed that the Beothuk hunters had
not long before left the site. Their hurried exodus left little
doubt in Captain Buchan's mind that Indians had sighted the
expedition party and they had quickly and quietly moved away.

As each day passed the men wearied. The transporting of
supplies and equipment was becoming more difficult. At this
point the crew left behind all but the bare essentials for survival.
This served the double purpose of lightening their load, and
hopefully have provisions for the return journey.

DAYS 20, 21, AND 22, FEBRUARY 9, 10 AND 11:
After three days overcoming many obstacles, the party spotted
several empty wigwams when they finally reached the "great
pond" (Red Indian Lake). This was the area where Mary March
had been captured. The camp had been deserted. At the edge of
the lake all three wigwams were intact but unoccupied. One
contained an Indian corpse, believed to have been the slain mate
of Mary March. He was surrounded by his worldly possessions,
amongst which was found monogrammed Peyton linen taken
from John's boat the year before.

In this area a scaffold was erected and Mary March's red
coffin, ornamented with copper fittings and breast plate, was
placed upon it, securely out of reach of animals. In the tent that
was pitched, to protect it, were placed her possessions and
numerous gifts and trinkets that were brought along to appease
her tribe. This part of Captain Buchan's mission was now complete. Plans were made for the return journey back to the ship.

DAYS 23 AND 24, FEBRUARY 12 AND 13:

Having seen traces of footprints in the general area, believed to be those of the natives, Captain Buchan decided to camp for a couple of days in order for his men to scout the shore of the "great pond," over thirty miles in length. He was still hopeful of falling in with some of the natives and reconciling their fears.

DAY 25, FEBRUARY 14:

A small party of men headed by Midshipman Waller and John were sent on a day's reconnaissance. Places were found where the natives had lived including a temporary wigwam which showed signs of having been recently occupied. Some traces of moccasin prints could be seen in the snow and in some places impressions of rackets (snowshoes), leading eastward.

DAY 26, FEBRUARY 15:

The hardships experienced by Captain Buchan's men were beginning to show on them. The long walk that the men were forced to make each day was causing lameness amongst some of them, including John, who was now lame in one foot. The increasing risks to the men and the dwindling of provisions induced Captain Buchan to reject the idea of further searches for the natives and return to the ship. The plan to scout a chain of marshes had to be abandoned in order to retrace their steps with expediency, back to the caches of food along the way.

DAY 27, FEBRUARY 16:

At daybreak the party set out on the return journey. By noon they had reached the head of the Exploits River.

DAY 28, FEBRUARY 17:

Following the contour of the river all day they came upon an earlier camp of theirs and stayed the night.

DAY 29, FEBRUARY 18:

The men continued to retrace their journey along the river.

DAY 30, FEBRUARY 19:

After another long trek along the riverbanks the party reached the place where the extra provisions were stored. The men ate and had a well earned rest.

DAY 31, FEBRUARY 20:
As Buchan was anxious to gain as much information as possible about the natives, he decided to split his party by sending thirteen of his crew members who were in poor physical condition along the river to the ship, in company with Midshipman Stanley. Buchan and John and the rest of the crew about twenty-one in number, took a different route. John, whose foot had healed, led the party through the Badger Bay watershed, a series of ponds and connecting marshes, that would lead them in a northeast direction to the coastline.

DAYS 32, 33, 34 AND 35 FEBRUARY 21, 22, 23 AND 24:
Striking into the country in order to scout the Badger Bay watershed and circuit Hodges Hills, to the crew members it appeared to be in the "middle of nowhere." The men foresaw a difficult tramp over rugged terrain. Frequently they came upon evidence that the natives had previously been in the area but nothing to indicate recent habitation. The severe cold, coupled with exertion and fatigue, was causing the marines to despair. They could see no end in sight. Good morale was waning. They became skeptical of John in his judgment and accused him loudly of leading them astray. To reassure them and to quell their fears he showed them traps bearing his name, set out in the trails, used by one of his trappers, an indication that they were nearing his trapper's tilt.

DAY 36, FEBRUARY 25:
John led the party to his tilt situated on the New Bay Great Pond. The men were assured now that only one more day's march would bring them to their brig anchored at Peter's Arm.

DAY 37 AND 38, FEBRUARY 26 AND 27:
In a last attempt to meet the natives before the journey ended, Captain Buchan decided that he, John and two crew members would scout the New Bay area, so often frequented by the Beothuks. The remainder of the crew set off to walk the last lap of their journey, to the brig where they had arrived that same day. It was midnight when the Buchan party of four arrived at the coast of the Southwest Arm of New Bay. Another five miles took them to the South Arm of New Bay, where they stayed overnight at a settler's home. A quick change in the weather and a rapid thaw made travelling very difficult.

DAY 39, FEBRUARY 28:
The four men set their course for Peter's Arm to board the ship. After crossing marshland, woods and ridges, John brought them out to the Exploits River directly opposite his Lower Sandy Point salmon fishing station. They stayed overnight at the station and travelled the remaining five miles to the ship at Peter's Arm on the fortieth day of the Journey.

Meanwhile Midshipman Stanley, in the trek along the river, arrived back at the ship with his charges the following day.[91] Their travelling had been slowed due to the condition of the ailing men. They had almost reached their destination when they were overcome with exhaustion and their physical strength was at a low ebb. To lighten their burdens a decision was made to abandon all extra food supplies and equipment that the men were carrying, to preserve their strength in order to get back to the ship.

Ten days later Buchan wrote in his report to the governor: "I am happy to report that [on] an expedition where so much was necessarily hazardous that no individual of the party has received any material injury, and those that were indisposed are now recovered or in a state of convalescence.... The occurrences are set forth sufficiently clear to enable Your Excellency to appreciate the infinite labour and difficulty attending this journey and that nothing has been omitted within my power for the attainment of the desirable object of my mission."[92] He also mentioned "John Peyton Jr. of whose unremitting zeal and attention and that of my officers no expression of mine can do sufficient justice."[93]

He added: "One of the Lieutenants, assisted by Mr. Peyton, made a map of all the country explored; but what became of it he could not tell."[94]

Peyton "accompanied this expedition as a volunteer and kept a journal of the same. On their arrival back to the ship Captain Buchan asked for and received his journal as well as all other notes taken at this time."[95]

It is to be regretted that John's journal and map has not been found over the years, for it would have proven invaluable to researchers today. His records show he was a learned person for the times, very concise and thorough, with an obsession to jot down every detail.

On John's return from the expedition he found his shipyard at Indian Point was progressing favourably. The schooner being built was the *Anne*. At this time, it was nearing completion with the exception of the rigging.

The captain and crew of the *Grasshopper* would not forget their association with John, and the expedition they had undertaken together. In gratitude to John, Captain Buchan offered the assistance of his crew in rigging John's new schooner. The offer was accepted.

After the opening of navigation the *Grasshopper* returned to St. John's. The schooner *Anne* was launched and taken to St. John's, under temporary sail. Notes of Thomas Peyton stated:

> [My father] had a schooner of about sixty or seventy tons built at Indian Point, Exploits River, built by Garrett Curtice. This schooner, after being launched was run to St. John's under her lower mast and was rigged under the superintendence of Captain Buchan, by the seamen of His Majesty's ship *Grasshopper*. I believe her builder Mr. Curtice was there at the time finishing up her spars, etc. No expense was spared in the outfit and she was put out of hand in regular man-o'-war shape.

He also described the vessel:

This vessel was rigged as fore-topsail schooner of that date [circa 1820]. That is fore-topmast, with fixed top gallant mast and royal mast, so as to allow the same to be easily sent below in stormy weather. Her sail forward consisted of: fore-and-aft fore-sail, top-sail, ratlines fitted with bluntlines, clue lines, clue garnets and bowlines, top gallant sail and flying royal; also a square fore-sail for lighter winds, forward free sail, jib and flying jib and fore-top-mast, studding sails, after mainsail and large gaff-topsail.

This vessel certainly proved its seaworthiness. After sailing it for several years, John sold it to Thomas Ashman of St. John's. "It made two trips to the icefields; on one of these trips she returned with a full cargo of fat [seal pelts]. Before selling her, she made a trip across the Atlantic with a cargo of fish. Captain Holly was Master at the time."[96]

Later in his life John often related to his sons the events of the unforgettable experiences of his journey with Captain Buchan. His son Thomas, who became a Deputy Land Surveyor, had the oppor-tunity of spending much time along the riverbanks, places often mentioned by his father. Especially did he remember his father speak of a huge copper cooking pot used by the *Grasshopper*'s crew, measuring nineteen inches in height and twenty inches in diameter, with a twenty-one-gallon capacity. His father had told him that the pot was left behind on the return lap of the journey when Midshipman Stanley, in order to spare the sick men of his crew, was forced to abandon "the ship's stores."[97] Thomas later sought out the spot, retrieved the copper pot and took it to his home at Twillingate. The copper is considerably blackened from its use over open wood fires, but the heads of the large rivets are plainly visible.[98]

The copper cooking pot from the HMS Grasshopper

It was apparent that the Beothuks accepted the return of the body of Mary March, along with the presents placed beside her, for it was later found to have been removed from its scaffold.

The Colonial Secretary, Lord Bathurst, writing Governor Hamilton from London concerning Buchan's expedition, said:

> ...The conduct of Captain Buchan affords an additional instance of the zeal and judgement of that officer in situation of no inconsiderable difficulty and delicacy, and although he has not succeeded in the actual object which he had in view, yet his failure is in no degree to be attributed to other than accidental causes.[99]

To commemorate Buchan's feat the only island in Red Indian Lake was named Buchan's Island, located at the northeast angle of the large lake.[100] The iron mining town nearby was also later given the name of Buchans.

The younger John Peyton also received recognition for his feats when the Blue Mountain Tolt was renamed Mount Peyton. Geologist Alexander Murray noted:

> ...called in honour of John Peyton, Esq., J.P. as overlooking the scene of many of his youthful adventures during the days of Beothuks or Red Indians of Newfoundland.[101]

The mountain's solid mass of granite has an elevation of 1,600 feet, the highest point of land along the northeast section of Newfoundland. Geographically the mountain is located approximately twenty-five miles southwest of Gander Lake. It is visible when travelling the stretch of the Trans-Canada Highway from Gander to Glenwood.

Mount Peyton

10

The Young English Pioneer
Settles Down

John, the young English woodsman, enjoying the freedom of outdoor life on the island for more than eight years, was now ready to settle down and make Newfoundland his permanent home. He was in love with the country and also in love with a Newfoundland girl. She was Eleanor Elizabeth Mahaney, daughter of Valentine and Elizabeth Mahaney, formerly of Carbonear, then living, at Exploits Burnt Island. Her father carried on a cod fishery. Eleanor was said to be beautiful and intelligent. The difference in their ages was considerable, for John was almost twice her age. Family legend has it that although she was so much younger, John had vowed to wait for her and someday take her for his bride.

Before his marriage, John planned a voyage home to England to spend a winter with his aging mother who was still living at Wimborne.

In the fall of 1821 he secured a passage on one of Slade's vessels, a brig carrying a full load of cargo for market. The brig's hold contained tierces (casks of forty-two-gallon capacity) of pickled salmon, casks of cod liver oil, wet bulk salted codfish and uncured seal pelts. It seemed poor judgment on the part of the brig's owners to store slippery seal pelts between the tierces and casks. Over halfway across the Atlantic the slippery pelts caused the vessel's cargo to shift badly. This adventurous journey was a memorable experience for John, a near-tragedy that almost cost him his life. John's son later wrote:

I often heard him speak of his voyage home, leaving Twillingate late in the fall, in a brig belonging to the Slades, Captain Pimer. She had a good run off the coast and when about half passage, on a fine night, blowing a strong breeze, a sudden squall struck the vessel. The cargo shifted in her hold and over she went on her beam ends. It was not blowing a gale of wind, just a fresh breeze, the moon shining and the vessel running along with all ordinary sail set. Then an extra flaw of wind striking her with a smart lop on the quarter and over she goes.

The Captain rushed down in the companionway as best he could and returned immediately with two sharp axes, kept there in case of emergency; handed one to the mate, ran alongside of the vessel, cut the weather laniards, and then two or three chops with the axes on the masts and they broke off like pipe stems. The ship then partly righted. First thing to be done was clear away the wreck which was done as quickly as possible under the circumstances; saving what spars, rigging and canvas they could. They got into the hold of the vessel and commenced righting up the cargo which consisted of salmon in tierces, oil in casks, and fish in bulk, also seal skins stowed in between casks.

During the morning the wind moderated off and going to work with a will they soon had the gerry masts rigged up and set sail again. A day or so after, a man-o'-war ship passing on the way, bore down on them asking if they required any assistance, which, after thanking them for their offer, replied "No," but giving the name of their vessel, asked to be reported, which after they arrived home they found had been done. I often heard him [my father] speak of that night. The first thought was [that] all [were] gone. Next seeing the energy and quickness of the captain, backed up by the mate and crew, hearing him say all right or we soon will be so. I heard him [my father] say he ran back aft and forward again on the ship's side just as well as he could walk on her deck in ordinary weather. She was not on her side very long.[102]

John returned to Newfoundland in the spring of 1822. During the mid-winter of 1823, when Eleanor Mahaney reached her seventeenth birthday and John was in his thirty-second year, they were married at Exploits Burnt island where they planned to settle.

Exploits Island and the surrounding areas were lacking both churches and clergymen, so the marriage ceremony of Eleanor and John was performed by a schoolteacher, William Mosdell, formerly of Brigus, then living at Exploits. Their handwritten marriage certificate reads:

> This is to certify that John Peyton, Jr. of Christchurch in Hampshire, England, now of the Bay of Exploits, Newfoundland, and Eleanor Mahaney of Exploits, Burnt Island, Newfoundland were married on the 21st of February 1823. No regular minister of the Church of England living within the limits of fifty miles and the said John Peyton, Jr. being one of the only two magistrates of the district, the said ceremony was performed by me.
>
> Signed: William Mosdell, late of Brigus now of Exploits. School Master, in the presence of Richard Rogers.

During the spring of that same year, John's elderly father, then aged seventy-six, made what was to be his final trip to England to visit his wife, returning to Newfoundland in the fall. His son John made the following note in his diary:

> Mr. John Peyton "the elder" arrived from England in the *Cornhill*, Captain Baggs, October 1823. Also Mr. John Owen, Mr. A. Owen and son, Trynmouth, Devon.

The elder John Peyton died four years later, aged eighty years, in August 1827 on the Exploits River at Upper Sandy Point. John Jr. had his father's body conveyed by boat to Exploits Burnt Island for burial, comparatively out of reach of any Beothuks who might still remain in the area.[103] The small graveyard, nestled low in the valley amidst the stark rocky outcroppings of the island, was not far from John and Eleanor's new home. The Beothuks, now numbering very few, no longer had to fear the old river lord, once their chief opponent on the river.

Meanwhile keels were laid for two square-rigged ships, one to be constructed at John's Exploits Island shipyard and the other at his shipyard at Indian Point. The ships were 150 tons each. One was named the *Worcester* and the other the *Amprilite*. The firm of Brooking and Company had an interest in the building and equipping of these vessels. The furnishings, namely sails, rigging, blocks and ropes for one of the vessels came from England, ready-made and fitted. Everything was destroyed in a fire at Brooking's stores with no insurance carried. Both brigs, when once more outfitted, sailed from Brooking House at St. John's with a full cargo on board and were never heard from again.

To John this was a tremendous loss and in the early 1830s he was forced to give up the business of shipbuilding. The superintendent of the shipbuilding yards, Garrett Curtice, sold his home and premises (fishing stage, fish-drying flakes and gardens) on Exploits Island to Thomas Colbourne of Sturminster, Newton, England for £25 and returned to his home at Salmonier.

It was during those same years that the inshore cod fishery failed in the Exploits area. Thomas Peyton wrote that his father

> ...fitted out his schooner *Anne*, then in her full bloom and sent her with a crew of fishermen to the French shore[104] at Fleur de Lys Harbour. On her arrival at that harbour there were several French fishing vessels there. Some of the fishing captains or the majority of them objected to my father's crew fishing. One of the captains who was acquainted with my father advised him to see the French Commodore. Immediately they sailed to Croque Harbour where the Commodore was situated and registered their complaint. He at once got his ship under way and sailed to Fleur de Lys accompanied by my father. Anchoring at the mouth of the harbour, a boat was sent in to the fishing captains who immediately came to the ship and both sides of the case were heard. After hearing the case, my father's schooner was given permission to fish and was to be assisted in any way possible. Francis Mahaney,[105] a fisherman in the crew said, "There was never a vessel more quickly filled up with green [uncured] fish as the French fishermen coming alongside and pitching the fish on board until their skipper cried 'Stop.'"

In his capacity as Justice of the Peace for the large area of the northern district, John had to do a lot of travelling along the coastline visiting settlers who sought advice and hearing disputes. This meant long periods away from home. The Peytons kept a maidservant, a widow named Mrs. Jure, who was company for Eleanor during John's absence.

On several occasions John was called to settle disputes between the English and French fishermen. The French, fishing only during the summer months, often had their premises destroyed in their absence and quantities of salt carried away.

Perhaps the most unusual episode in John's capacity as Justice of the Peace happened a few months after his marriage in the same year, 1823. Three Beothuk women who had been wandering in starving condition in the New Bay area gave themselves up to a fur trapper named William Cull. He brought them to Exploits Island and left them in John's charge. One of them was Shanawdithit.

11

Shanawdithit (Nancy April)

She crept along the riverbank,
With every little noise she shrank.
Her face contorted with a fear
Of enemies she knew not where.
At last, so driven with despair
She went into a camp and there
Pleaded for a mercy not shown
To other folks of her own.
The Gods were kind to her that day
And with the younger John she'd stay,
Until some curious city folk
Showed her unfamiliar city ways...[106]

Shanawdithit, when found in the early spring of 1823, was accompanied by her sister and aging mother. They were wandering in the New Bay area, separated from the rest of their tribe. The women had been unable to fend for themselves after the only male of their band had fallen through the ice and drowned a few weeks before. They were without food and in a starving condition. William Cull, who came upon the three of them while visiting his traplines, recognized their plight.

Cull, knowing the younger John Peyton's concern for the natives and his obligation as a government official to protect them, felt these three women should be turned over to John's charge. He brought them to the Peyton home on Exploits Burnt Island. Food was immediately given them and a shelter, in the form of a tilt, was erected near John's home. This allowed the natives to live as they wished, and they had freedom to go and come as they desired.

The mother of the two young Beothuk women was prematurely old. She apparently was unattractive and did not impress John's workmen in the shipyard, who dubbed her "Old Smut."

Shanawdithit was young, about twenty years of age. She stood an average height. Her complexion was swarthy and her hair was jet black and coarse in texture. Her face was broad with high cheekbones. She was gentle in manner and seemed to be intelligent. She appeared to be strong and healthy, despite being half-starved.[107]

The other girl was much younger than her sister Shanawdithit and was very frail.

While the natives lived at Exploits Island the mother was often seen heating large stones, on which she would throw water to create steam around her young daughter. This "steam bath" was believed to have been an attempt at a remedy for her illness. No doubt it proved useful to suppress the persistent cough of consumption, as her condition was diagnosed shortly thereafter.

With the opening of navigation in June 1823, John had the three women taken to St. John's to await further instructions from Governor Hamilton, who still wished for reconciliation with the natives. They sailed to St. John's on the *Anne*. On their arrival at St. John's it was found that the governor was away. Captain Buchan, who acted as the governor's deputy in his absence, solicited the services of Dr. Watt, surgeon of the HMS *Grasshopper*, to attend the women's health. The condition of the mother and younger daughter was thought to be rather precarious; the girl was in an advanced stage of consumption.

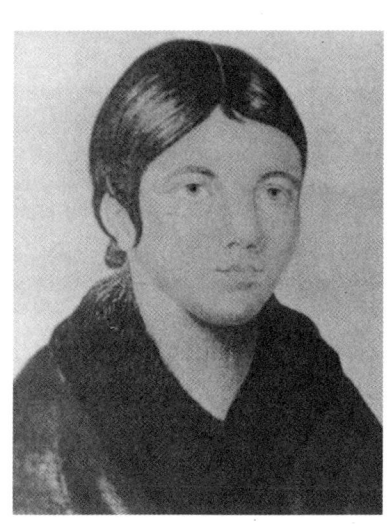

Beothuk native Shanawdithit

The authorities felt that it was imperative to return the natives to their own environment. The Beothuks were given food and gifts. Ten days later they were taken by John, as he had been directed, to a place as near as possible to where they had been found. The instructions from Captain Buchan had been:

> As it appears to me in every point of view of the first consideration that the three female aborigines should be conducted with the least possible delay to such station as may enable them with the less difficulty to rejoin their tribe. I feel most desirous on behalf of His Excellency the Governor to facilitate this pleasing object, and it is particularly gratifying to me that my personal knowledge of your humanity, zeal and ability qualified you in an eminent degree for this confidence and trust which I impose on you under a perfect conviction that your proceedings herein will

prove most satisfactory to His Majesty's Government. You will, therefore, again take charge of the three native females with the presents enumerated in the annexed schedule, which you will use as circumstances and your discretion may render most suit-able as an incitement to these poor creatures to repose confi-dence in our people on that part of the coast they frequent.

It is impossible to give adequate written instructions on a subject that must even vary according to the circumstances of the movement, and as you are perfect master of what were my intentions and view in the expeditions of 1819 and 1820, it ren-ders it altogether unnecessary for me to say anything on these heads. Should you, however, find it necessary to carry your oper-ations to any part of the coast not included between the NW. entrance of the Exploits, tracing up the Western side of that bay by Charles Brook to the River Exploits, you will leave at Exploits Burnt Island, also at Twillingate, a letter of instruction where you may be found...[108]

On John's return home by schooner to Exploits Bay, he immediately carried out the instructions he had received from Captain Buchan. He landed the three natives with food and supplies, on July 12, 1823 at Charles Brook, where there was an unoccupied wigwam. John wrote, "They appeared perfectly happy at our leaving them."[109] Two days later, on July 14, John, in his concern for the natives, again visited the area. They were still there but the younger sister showed signs of being grave-ly ill.

John left one of his "flats" for their use, at which "Shanawdithit was much pleased." John had many such small boats that he referred to as "flats"; lightweight, flat bottom, square ends, which he himself had always used and found to be invaluable for cruising the shallow brooks and for easy portage. He believed that Shanawdithit would be better able to get far-ther inland by way of the brooks, and would more easily be able to meet up with her people. He hoped she would establish a friendly association with the last of the Beothuks. It seemed a strange decision for Buchan and John to have made, to leave the natives, but the hope was that an amicable meeting with the Beothuks might be accomplished.

A very short time afterwards the younger daughter died. Shanawdithit and her mother paddled their "flat" from Charles Brook down the north side of Exploits Bay, in sheltered waters across the short distance of the bay from Point-of-Bay to Peyton's salmon station and premises at Lower Sandy Point. They were quite familiar with that area and this salmon station, for a few years previously they had been members of the tribe which had cut John's boat adrift. Here Mr. Pike and several of John's men operated the cooperage. Shanawdithit sought their help. She said her sister was "winum," meaning asleep, or dead. The men went to Charles Brook and buried the girl's body.

While at Lower Sandy Point the mother also died and was buried. Shanawdithit was taken to Exploits Island where John and Eleanor Peyton accepted her into their household. They called her Nancy and she was often referred to as Nancy April (from the month in which she was taken), or "Indian Nance."

Shanawdithit helped Mrs. Jure with the simple household chores that she was capable of doing. She was not treated as an ordinary servant and so was allowed to come and go as she pleased. Quite often she became melancholy and would wander off into the woods nearby staying for several days at a time. Here she supposedly, according to her own accounts, communicated with the spirits of her "winum" mother and sister. After such seances she would return to the Peyton home in a happier frame of mind.

Some accounts have stated that Shanawdithit lived in obscurity in the Peyton kitchen for five years. The Governor of Newfoundland knew she was there, as did all other authorities. During those five years no one other than members of the Peyton household attempted to learn more about her people, learn her language or teach her any skills. She learned some English from Eleanor and John, and Mrs. Jure. James Howley noted, "She had acquired considerable knowledge of English from them."[110] Although she spoke in phrases of broken English she was easily understood. Mrs. Gill, a former servant of the Peytons, quoted Shanawdithit as saying, "All gone 'winum', Nance go 'winum' too, no more come Nance, run away, no more come."[111]

During the five years of Shanawdithit's stay with the Peyton's at Exploits, Eleanor Peyton bore three children. Her first-born was named Ann, the second was named John III, referred to as John Henry, and the third child died in infancy. As the young family grew, Shanawdithit assumed a much different role. She helped Eleanor with the care of the children and grew especially fond of them. She often rocked them, and they often looked to her for care and comfort.

The Reverend Canon Walter R. Smith, in his notes on *Church and Secular History of Notre Dame Bay*, wrote: "The Bishop had two or three interviews with Shanawdithit who was then a member of Mr. Peyton's family." He wrote of

Shanawdithit, "She is fond of children, who leave their mother and go to her."

Captain Buchan showed an interest in Shanawdithit, supplying her with pencils and paper, when she was first brought to St. John's. It was found she possessed a talent for sketching, and made a sketch of Captain Buchan's mother from a portrait he had shown her. While living at Exploits, Captain Buchan sent her a gift of stockings and a pair of shoes, "in which she took great pride."[112]

Shanawdithit showed a great dislike and dread of the Mi'kmaq Indians. She had an unforgettable encounter with one of the Mi'kmaq tribe. Shots were fired, and this had heightened her fears. At the sight of one of them she was terrified, screaming and clinging to John for protection.[113]

Another fear, a common belief of her tribe, was that some powerful monster or demon would appear from the "great waters," the sea, to punish the wicked.[114]

While living in the Peyton home Eleanor and John did not attempt to convert Shanawdithit to Christianity. Shanawdithit must have experienced heart-rending loneliness as probably the last survivor of her people. If she received solace and fulfillment from her own method of worship, in communication with her "winum" relatives, why deny her that privilege? At any rate, the Peytons did not prevent her from following her own beliefs.

Bishop Inglis, during his visit to John's home in 1827, thought otherwise. He criticized John for not schooling Shanawdithit in the doctrines of the Church of England, in preparation for a Christian baptism and confirmation.[115]

12

A Visit from Bishop Inglis

During the early 1800s, the Society for the Propagation of the Gospel, to establish the Church of England in Newfoundland, sent from England a small number of clergy to preach the gospel and to establish churches and schools. The Church of England ministry on the island in 1827 consisted of only eight resident clergymen. They were stationed at intervals along the 600-mile stretch of the eastern coastline. The sparsely populated southern coast of the island had not yet a single resident clergyman. The diocese of Newfoundland came under the jurisdiction of the Bishop of Nova Scotia, the Right Reverend John Inglis.

Bishop Inglis was born at New York, NY but studied for the ministry at King's College in Windsor, Nova Scotia.

The settlements in the provinces of Nova Scotia and New Brunswick came under his jurisdiction, as well as the distant islands of the Bermudas and the island of Newfoundland, "that remote part of the diocese." Bishop Inglis planned a visit to Newfoundland in the summer of 1827 to acquaint himself with his new mission. The Admiralty of the Halifax naval station placed at His Lordship's disposal HMS *Orestes* for his visitation to Newfoundland. The *Orestes* was commanded by a Captain Jones of the Royal Navy. The ship left Halifax on May 24, 1827 and reached St. John's four days later.

On arrival at St. John's harbour Bishop Inglis made the following entry in his diary:

> The entrance to the harbour of St. John's is highly picturesque. It is a strait, so narrow that large vessels must be warped[116] in, if the wind is not favourable, between fortified heights that rise almost perpendicularly, and nearly 600 ft. above water. Close to the entrance an iceberg was grounded in 66 fathoms of water, and with nearly 200 ft. of its mass above the surface.[117]

Reverend William Bullock, missionary at Trinity Bay, was His Lordship's chaplain during the Newfoundland tour. After consecrating St. John's Church and holding services there and in other nearby settlements of the Avalon peninsula, Bishop Inglis and his party left St. John's, June 8, on the *Orestes* to visit parishes and missions to the northward. They reached Toulinguet (Twillingate), which was considered the "Capital of the North" on June 30. A consecration of St. Peter's Church and burial grounds took place. The *Orestes* then left for Exploits Burnt Island. Reverend Chapman, rector of St. Peter's, accompanied the bishop on this part of the journey.

At Exploits Burnt Island the bishop's party was met and welcomed by John Peyton. Bishop Inglis mentions him in his entry of July 2, 1827: "Mr. Peyton, the principal magistrate of the place, [met us] and [is] a very intelligent person."[118] John

Peyton wrote in his diary for July 2, 1827: "HMS *Orestes* arrived off L.B. Isle [Little Burnt Isle] with the Bishop of Nova Scotia and suite."[119] Also in John's diary were the following navigational directions he had prepared for the captain:

Lat. Cape Charles 52 12" Long. 55 31;
Lat. Phillip's Brook, Bay of Exploits,
Lat. 49 14-10, N. Long. 55 12 30w.;
Exploits Burnt Island
Long. 54 58 30w.

HMS *Orestes*, Capt. Jones, R.N. 1827.

He also jotted down the captain's address as "Capt. Jones R.N. To care Messers. Barrett and Ring, 37 Essex Street, South West End, London."

The bishop and his party were taken to John's home, where they were hospitably entertained by Eleanor and John. Bishop Inglis had heard of the Beothuk natives of the island and knew the sad possibility of the extinction of the Beothuk tribe. While visiting John's home the bishop met Shanawdithit.

Shanawdithit was able to communicate only minimally with the bishop. In his interviews with her, he made the following deductions and observations:

She is fond of his [John Peyton's] children, who leave their mother to go to her, and soon learned all that was necessary to make her useful in the family. Her progress in the English language has been slow, and I greatly lamented to find that she had not received sufficient instruction to be baptized and confirmed... She is now twenty-three years old, very interesting, rather graceful, and of a good disposition; her countenance mild, and her voice soft and harmonious. Sometimes a little sullenness appears, and an anxiety to wander, when she will pass twenty-four hours in the woods, and return; but this seldom occurs. She is fearful that her race has died from want of food. Mr. Peyton has learnt from her that the traditions of the Beothick [sic] represent their descent from the Labrador Indians, but the language of one is wholly unintelligible to the other.[120]

Later, at a confirmation service held at Exploits Burnt Island, the bishop noted:

Shanawdithit was present. She perfectly understood that we were engaged in religious services, and seemed struck with their solemnity. Her whole deportment was serious and becoming. She was also made to understand my regret that her previous instruction had not been as to allow of her baptism and confirmation, and my hope and expectation that she would be well prepared if it should please God that we meet again. Mr Peyton pledged himself that every possible endeavour should be made for this purpose.[121]

The following day John escorted Bishop Inglis and party on a boat excursion up the picturesque, untamed Exploits River to view the magnificent waterfall. Of this occasion the bishop entered the following in his diary for July 3, 1827:

This was the first day since I left Halifax that was devoted to personal gratification. The weather was fine, but as hot as I have ever felt.... We went in the boats about thirteen miles up the river to a rapid, where we landed, and walked about two miles to a splendid waterfall. The land is good, finely wooded with large timber, and the scenery is rich and picturesque. Mr. Peyton, who was with us, has twelve fishing stations for salmon along thirty miles of river, and the abundance of seal, deer, wild fowl, and game of every description is surprising. But our interest in all we saw was greatly increased by knowing that this was the retreat of the Beothuk or red, or wild Indians, until the last four or five years. We were on several of their stations and saw many of their traces.[122]

John entered in his diary for that day: "Accompanied them up the Exploits. Visited Bishop's Falls, River Exploits."

The bishop was most impressed by the beauty of the area and especially by the grandeur of the falls. The falls, and later the town, in close proximity to it, has retained the name of Bishop's Falls. During the 1970s, almost 150 years later, the high school at Bishop's Falls was named the Inglis Memorial, in commemoration of the bishop's first visit.

This waterfall impressed many people. Captain David Buchan in his journal of March 1811 had written:

> The sight repaid the trouble of getting to it. The scene was truly interesting; the upper part was formed by a number of cascades, and at last joining their united streams, rolled down one stupendous height of at least eight feet perpendicular.

While at Exploits Island the bishop noted that Mr. William Mosdell, "a competent person of good character," was recommended as School Master, Sunday School teacher and church layman, with a salary allowance of £15, to be paid yearly by the Society of Propagation of the Gospel. It was this same William Mosdell who had performed the marriage ceremony of John and Eleanor four years earlier when no clergy was available.

As Exploits was considered the northern frontier of this island, in close proximity to Cape John, the border of the French fishing territories, the *Orestes* left on its return journey the next day for St. John's. Bishop Inglis later joined the HMS *Alligator* under the command of Captain Canning, for the return voyage to Halifax.

While at St. John's, Bishop Inglis was contacted by William E. Cormack, who described his journey across the island of Newfoundland in 1822 and who requested the bishop's opinion on his plans for another journey for that fall of 1827.

13

Association with Cormack

William Epps Cormack was born in Newfoundland of Scottish parents and educated at the Universities of Edinburgh and Glasgow in Scotland in the fields of botany, geology and mineralogy. He had a love of the outdoors and the wilderness. His wanderings and schemes were both varied and widespread. He never seemed to continue at one thing or stay in one place for long. His father's wealth allowed him to be "footloose and fancy-free." He travelled all over the world and dabbled in such ventures as transporting immigrants from Scotland to Prince Edward Island, growing tobacco in Australia, raising horses and cattle in New Zealand, mining in California, agriculture in British Colombia and other endeavours.

In Newfoundland he is noted mostly for his journey on foot across the breadth of the island in 1822 with a lone Mi'kmaq Indian guide name Joe Sylvester. Many have claimed Cormack made this journey in search of the dwindling tribe of Beothuk Indians. Others argue that they could not possibly have found any Beothuks. His Mi'kmaq guide, fearful of the Island natives, steered Cormack to the southward, far remote from Beothuk territory. This apparently was not realized by Cormack until the journey's end. Not a Beothuk was sighted during the entire journey, nor were any traces of them discovered.

Cormack published detailed accounts of his undertakings, giving his interpretations of his journeys and endeavours to *The London Times*, *The Edinburgh New Philosophical Journal*, The Linnean Society, Montreal Natural History Society, Agricultural Society of British Columbia and the local *Royal Gazette*, *The Newfoundlander*, and *The Public Ledger*.

During Cormack's journey across the island his knowledge of botany proved useful as he made detailed observations on the island flora. His knowledge of geology and mineralogy raised the possibility that good sources of mineral would be found in areas formerly uncharted.

Cormack often visited the home of Eleanor and John Peyton. Eleanor once described him as "a long-legged, wiry but eccentric individual who could eat almost everything."[123]

By the mid-1820s it was well known that the Beothuk tribe had dwindled drastically. It was even feared the tribe was reaching a point of extinction. Cormack was anxious to discover if this was so. In 1827 he planned another trek into the heart of the interior of the island, this time farther to the northward, the area already known to be Beothuk territory. Cormack hoped that John Peyton would accompany him on this trip, but this did not happen. Apparently John, with the information already acquired from Shanawdithit, fearful that her race had died from want of food,[124] thought such a journey to be futile.

Judge Des Barres of St. John's knew of Cormack's plans and his desire to get to Notre Dame Bay in the general vicinity of the Exploits River. Des Barres, travelling on the northern court circuit, planned court sessions at Twillingate for September 11, 1827. A schooner was the only way of travelling around the island, and Judge Des Barres offered Cormack passage travel on his vessel to Twillingate to allow Cormack "to facilitate the very humane and praiseworthy expedition in contemplation."[125]

William Cormack's sister was married to Reverend John Chapman and lived at Twillingate, where her husband was stationed at St. Peter's Parish during that time (1827-1843). During a visit with the Chapmans that fall, Cormack was able to make plans for his second journey. Cormack wrote John Peyton (apparently his second letter) from Twillingate:[126]

OCT. 5, 1827

I duly received your esteemed favour of the 2nd inst. with its enclosures. I assure you it gives me sincere regret that you cannot join me in my intended visit to the Red Indians this fall, but in the winter of 1828 and 1829 Mr. Thos. Slade has offered to join yourself and I [sic] in an excursion to see them, and we must keep such an excursion in view.

My object this fall will only be to see some of them, leave a favourable impression with them of the friendly disposition of some white people. If this is done and they are not molested for a year afterwards, we will be likely to have a friendly interview with them with some confidence existing between the parties.

I go to Gander [meaning Gander Bay] tomorrow with Mr. Thos. Slade to procure two more good Indians [Mi'kmaq], and then proceed with them all to Exploits to take our departure from some place. Should Joseph Sylvester [former guide] come your way, if he knows where to find the Indians I would like very well he would travel with me again.... If I should not have the pleasure to see you before, I hope to have it after my return from my expedition. Call on my people at St. John's.

My dear Sir,
In haste, Yours faithfully,
W.E. Cormack.

Probably the references to "favour" and "enclosures" meant information and maps of the terrain.

It was also that fall, while at Twillingate, that Cormack thought of creating a "Beothuk Institution" with its first objective being "that of bringing about a reconciliation of the Aborigines, to the approaches of civilization." Cormack proposed this, and it was unanimously resolved at the first meeting to make Bishop Inglis of Nova Scotia the Honorary Patron of the Institution and Professor Jameson of Scotland an Honorary Vice-Patron.

The first meeting of the Beothuk Institution was held in the courthouse at Twillingate on October 2, 1827. The meeting was chaired by Judge Des Barres, and William Cormack became the Institution's first President and Treasurer; John Stark was to be Secretary. Along with twelve others who were proposed as corresponding members of the Institution, John Peyton was corresponding member for Exploits.

At this meeting a proposal of thanks was put forward by Cormack:

That the thanks of this meeting are due, and hereby given, to John Peyton, Esq. for valuable information afforded by him; and that he be requested to continue to use his best endeavours to promote the humane objects of this institution.[127]

Another proposal made at this meeting was:

That Shanawdithit be placed under the paternal care of the Institution: the expense of her support and education to be provided for out of general funds.[128]

In a letter to John Peyton from Cormack concerning this meeting, he wrote on October 5, 1827, from Twillingate:

We have formed an Institution here called "The Beothuk Institution" for reclaiming the Red Indians. The Bishop of Nova Scotia, Judge Des Barres, myself, Mr. Dunscrombe and son [believed to have been travelling with the judge] and many others, belong to it. You are agent and corresponding member at Exploits. Funds to support it and promote its objects are to be raised next year. The particulars of the Institute are to be published this fall.[129]

Meanwhile Cormack, in previous contact with Bishop Inglis, sought his opinion of his proposed expedition into the interior. The bishop advised if remnants of the tribe were to be found, the searchers should be kept few in number, suggesting Cormack, John Peyton, Shanawdithit and two guides.

Shortly afterwards, Cormack was successful in obtaining the services of three Mi'kmaq Indians to accompany him on his proposed journey. He proceeded from Twillingate to Exploits where he visited the home of John Peyton. By October 31, the party of four [Cormack and the three Micmacs] was ready and equipped to start their journey and entered the country on the north side of the Exploits River

near Northern Arm. On leaving John's house, Cormack was
described by John as "a lithe, active robust man." The journey
into the interior lasted thirty days. When Cormack returned
from his expedition and revisited John's home, John could
scarcely recognize him for he had changed so much.

> He presented such a gaunt, haggard and worn-out appearance
> from the excessive toil and privation he had undergone, accom-
> panied by hunger and anxiety, that he did not look much like the
> stalwart individual [I] saw depart for the interior a month pre-
> viously.[130]

The journey to Red Indian Lake had been very arduous. En
route they encountered many signs of deserted encampments
and traces of Beothuks now believed to be long gone. In the
vicinity of Red Indian Lake the party discovered the remains
of Mary March, removed from the scaffold where it had been
placed by Captain Buchan and John, and placed in a wooden
repository for Indian dead. Inside the repository were
entombed several bodies, some wrapped in deerskins, Beothuk-
fashion and one wrapped in white muslin in a board coffin,
European-fashion—the body of Mary March. Inside the coffin
Cormack found two wooden images which "Peyton says were
so placed, along with several other articles she took a fancy to
while at St. John's, by Buchan's people."[131]

Cormack returned to St. John's. After writing his report of
the journey for the Beothuk Institution for presentation at the
meeting of January 12, 1828, he left for England to spend the
winter, leaving St. John's on the brigantine *George Canning* on
January 10.

Cormack returned again to Newfoundland in May, 1828. He kept in frequent contact with Bishop Inglis, telling him of his plans, and in reply the bishop gave his reviews on such matters. It was characteristic of Cormack that he would solicit the bishop's opinion and influential support in many of his endeavours.

The Beothuk Institution intended to raise funds by public subscription during the summer for the education and maintenance of Shanawdithit.

> *At last, but too late, they searched in vain.*
> *Shanawdithit's folks she'd never see again.*
> *Conscience had spoken, but too late*
> *To save these people from their fate.*[132]

14

Shanawdithit in St. John's

Again they come to carry me away
There is no one for to say them nay,
To take me far, far out to sea,
To point and laugh at my curiosity.
If only my kind master were at home,
For he would understand, and he alone
Would stand between their demands and me.[133]

During the same summer that the Beothuk Institution was raising funds for Shanawdithit's education, Cormack made plans to have Shanawdithit removed from John's charge and taken to St. John's, so that he could learn her language and to further instruct her in the English language.

John Stark, the Secretary of the Beothuk Institution, was sent to Twillingate in the fall of 1828 by Cormack for the purpose of bringing Shanawdithit (Nancy) back to St. John's by schooner. From Twillingate a yacht was sent to Exploits Island to get her, but it had to leave without her. Eleanor Peyton was reluctant to let them take Nancy away without her husband's knowledge and consent.[134]

Four days later, on September 12, 1828, Eleanor, probably after giving the matter much thought and consideration, sent Nancy by boat to Reverend and Mrs. Chapman at Twillingate to start the journey to St. John's. John Stark, when writing to Cormack of the incident, said:

> ...I ought to say that Mrs. Peyton [Eleanor] was quite willing for her to come away and I hope Mr. Peyton [John] will not be displeased. To please Nancy I shall give her a separate note to you...[135]

Apparently John, on his arrival home, was indeed much displeased. He had accepted the Beothuk native into his family, had fed and clothed her for five years. His children were fond of her and she of them, and she had adjusted well to their way of life.

John was upset, not because he was losing a servant, but because of a new upheaval in Shanawdithit's life which had taken place without his knowledge. Cormack, as a friend, had often accepted the hospitality of John and Eleanor. Now John had not been informed by Cormack of his intentions, and John wanted to know why. His inquiry to the governor brought the following reply from T. Holdworth Brooking, aide-de-camp to Sir Thomas Cochrane, written on October 28, 1828:

> I understand His Excellency had nothing to do with the removal of the Indian woman, Nancy, but she had been brought here solely under the directions of those who formed an institution for some purpose which I apprehend they now can accomplish.... In your absence nothing can be done towards obtaining satisfaction in respect to any claim which you may prefer against those who removed your charge, and the business had better remain for consideration until spring when you visit St. John's and you may assert your own rights...[136]

John's inquiry to Cormack brought an ingratiating reply, written on October 28, 1828:

> ...Nancy arrived in St. John's by Mr. Abbott's schooner from Twillingate on the 28th of last month. We were hardly prepared to receive her just then, altho' we ought to have been, for besides what took place here last winter on the subject, when you were here in summer, there was a good deal said about bringing her round to instruct her, and it was intended to mention it to you as a proposition, but it was delayed day after day until you had gone. I am certain you would have coincided in opinion with us in thinking it highly proper as well as incumbent on the people of Newfoundland and have her instructed; and I know that you would have given every facility in your power to promote this object by sending her round here. Your being absent when she came away from your place was quite an accidental thing and under the circumstances you must consider that every thing was done for the best, and with the best intentions. She has been staying in my house since she came, but leaves next week to live with Mr. Simms, the Attorney General, who has undertaken to superintend her instructions. Much is due to you and Mrs. Peyton for taking care of this woman so long as you have.... P.S. Nancy sends your family a few marks of remembrance.[137]

The note that John Stark gave Shanawdithit to take to Cormack read:

> This note will I trust be handed to you by the Red Indian Shanawdithit herself. She asked me if you had any family, I told her that when I left St. John's you were single but that I could not tell how long you would remain so. Above all things I request you will get her vaccinated by Dr. Carson upon the very day she reaches St. John's, pray let nothing prevent this.[138]

Stark wrote another letter to Cormack of September 16:

> ...I should by all means recommend her being immediately placed under the care of some steady woman and placed in

school every day.... She wants [needs] new clothes.... Let me suggest that a stout watch should always be kept over her morals
and that no one should be allowed to see her without special
permission...[139]

Although such a warning had been given Cormack, short-
ly after Shanawdithit's arrival in St. John's, the *Royal Gazette* of
October 21, 1828 printed:

Those who are curious in enquiries relating to man have a treat
just now in St. John's such as is not likely again to be met with.
There are at present at Mr. Cormack's house, accessible at all
times to those who feel an interest, individuals belonging to
three different tribes of North American Indians via a
Mountaineer [Montagnais] from Labrador, two of the Banakee
[Abenaki] nation from Canada, and a Beothuk, or Red Indian of
Newfoundland, the last, a female. They all speak different lan-
guages and are good specimens of the race.

The Montagnais and two Abenaki Indians were Cormack's
former guides who had recently returned from a search for the
Beothuks in the White Bay area.

Shanawdithit had become a public spectacle. The shy young
woman was exposed to public scrutiny and curiosity. She was
unaccustomed to being treated as an object rather than a person. Shanawdithit's inherent fear of the Mi'kmaq must have
caused her great anxiety and terror at their presence in
Cormack's household.

She probably had felt apprehension on having to leave the
Peyton family. She was now unable to be part of the warmth of
a family, had no female company, and undoubtedly missed the
affections of the young Peyton children.

Again Cormack wrote to Bishop Inglis on October 26, commenting:

> The Red Indian woman Shanawdithit has been at length brought to St. John's and for the present is staying at my house.... Shanawdithit is to leave me in a week or two to stay with Mr. Simms the Attorney General. This gentleman has been one of the warmest advocates here for humanity towards her people and I know it will be a gratification to him to take care of her and have her instructed.... She is already a faithful domestic servant...[140]

After only five to six weeks Cormack passed on his responsibilities towards Shanawdithit to the Attorney General, Mr. Simms. His desire for greater adventure was now taking his attention. He wrote Bishop Inglis on January 10, 1829:

> Shanawdithit is now becoming very interesting as she improves in the English language, and gains confidence in people around. I keep her pretty busily employed in drawing historical representations of everything that suggests itself relating to her tribe, which I find is the best and readiest way of gathering information from her. She has also nearly completed making a dress of her tribe.... I expect to sail to England about the end of the month, and may not return here again...[141]

Shanawdithit's contribution in teaching Cormack some of the language and customs of her people must be weighed against the probable harm done to her physical and mental health in removing her from a familiar environment to the public, but lonely, life in St. John's.

She lived for about eight months with Mr. Simms, but her health declined and later became consumptive. She died in hospital of tuberculosis on June 6, 1829, nine months after being moved to St. John's. Her remains were buried in the Church of England cemetery on the South Side of St. John's two days later, on June 8. The Cathedral Parish Register recorded:

> Interred Nancy, Shanawdithe [sic] at South Side (Very probably the last of the aborigines).
>
> Signed: Frederick H. Carrington, A.B. Rector,
> St. John's

The Public Ledger of June 12, 1829, contains the following:

> Died--On Saturday night of the 6th inst. at the hospital, Shanawdithit, the female Indian, one of the aborigines of this island, probably the last of the native Indians. Since the departure of Mr. Cormack from the island, the poor woman has had an asylum afforded her in the house of James Simms, Esq., Attorney General, where every attention has been paid to wants and comfort, and under the able professional advice of Dr. Carson, who has been most kindly and liberally attending her for many months past, it was hoped that her health might have been re-established.

Unfortunately, over the years the whereabouts of the grave of Shanawdithit (Nancy) have been completely forgotten. In recent years a plaque has been erected in what is believed to be the general vicinity of her gravesite.

In a business letter to John Peyton of June 12, 1829, four days after Shanawdithit's burial, John Kent of the business firm of J. and J. Kent wrote:

> Before this reaches [you] I suppose you will have heard of the death of the Indian woman, Nancy. She died of consumption and the medical men of the town for the benefit of science dissected her body. Hoping to hear from you...[142]

An article in the *Evening Telegram* of May 26, 1956, entitled "A Vanished Race," said in part:

> Perish the thought that this autopsy, after death from consumption, was conducted by the doctors to satisfy their curiosity, as to whether or not the aborigines were "in form and feature, face and limb" different from other human beings.

Following Shanawdithit's death, John and Eleanor were again to hear from Cormack. The letter was written from London, England. He wrote:

> I was very sorry to hear of the death of poor Nancy. It is too much to be feared that we will hear nothing more of the remnant of her tribe. I have it not in my power yet to make any return for your civility to me when at Exploits but hope some time to have the pleasure to do so.... I hope Mrs. Peyton and your young family and friends continue well, and I remain dear sir,
>
> > Yours very truly
> > W.E. Cormack.[143]

The friendship of Cormack and John had deteriorated. In 1836 Cormack's roamings took him to Australasia, growing tobacco in Australia and raising horses and cattle in New Zealand, far remote from Exploits Burnt Island where John was raising his young family. John's steadiness and good character were admired and led to his promotion in the judicial department in 1836, when he was appointed Stipendiary Magistrate for the district of Twillingate and Fogo.

15

Twillingate's First Magistrate

John had worked twenty-four years cruising the River Exploits and sailing around the coastlines in the course of his duties. For him this was a fulfilling pursuit, but it was a difficult life for his growing family.

His appointment to Stipendiary Magistrate, made by Governor Sir Thomas Cochrane, was the first appointment of it's kind for the islands of Twillingate and Fogo. It meant that

he could have a more settled life in the community of Twillingate. He was not required to relinquish his salmon fishing rights of the Exploits River, and his business continued under his guidance as before.

John was well acquainted with the island of Twillingate, having spent time there in his line of duty

John Peyton "the Younger" when he was a magistrate

as Justice of the Peace. His friends there, the Slades and Owens, were two of the principal merchants. John Peyton was appointed to take a census of the area in 1832, the first census in the area to be recorded. The population that year in an area from Cape John to Cape Freels was 3,694.[144] He also took a second census in 1836, a more detailed one with statistical data. John received a letter concerning this latter census. It is addressed to John Peyton, Esq., Harbour Exploits:

MAY 11, 1836

Sir,
The Governor having under the authority of an Act passed during the late session of the Colonial Legislature been pleased to appoint you to take the census of the District of Fogo, extending from Fogo to Cape John, including Fogo and all other islands within those limits and to obtain the other statistical information required by said act.... The population of each settlement within the limits assigned to you, is to be inserted a recapitulation of the whole, showing the entire population of the District.... For the performance of the above duty to which His Excellency relies will not only be zealously and diligently executed, but completed with as much dispatch as circumstances will admit, you will be allowed the sum of 60.

I am, Sir
Your obedient servant,
signed: J. Templeman, Acting Secretary

P.S. You are to be duly sworn to the faithful performance thereof.

The swearing-in letter written at Twillingate reads:

John Peyton, Esq., J.P. of Exploits Island has this day appeared and taken the oath for the faithful performance of the duty assigned

him for taking the census of the population of the District of
Fogo and Twillingate agreeably to the Act.

                              Signed: Robert Tremblett, J.P.

Robert Tremblett was Twillingate's first medical doctor,
and Andrew Pearce a sub-collector of Customs.

The 1836 census shows the population of Twillingate
Islands as 1,315, consisting of 194 heads of households, 175
listed as "planters" and nineteen others. These were listed as
seven dealers, two agents, two ship's carpenters, a surgeon,
minister, constable, schoolteacher, tailor, blacksmith, customs
collector and an accountant.

There were 6,383 bushels of potatoes grown during that
year, an average of thirty-three bushels per family. There were
also 125 head of cattle and eighty hogs. The family statistics
list 1,260 Church of England adherents, nineteen Catholics
and thirty-six Protestant dissenters.

John had a large two-storey house built on a prime piece of
fertile land in the Back Harbour of Twillingate North Island,
overlooking a picturesque, deep water cove and beach. Most of
the land was cleared and made into potato and kitchen gardens,
hay meadows and grazing pastures for the cattle and other
livestock. A wooded portion was carefully preserved at the rear
of his property, and it is still known as Peyton's Woods. He
received his land grant in 1841.

John was a respected member of the community and made
many friends. He also played an active part in the community
and church life.[145]

"Planters" were establishing "fishing rooms" and premises on both the north and south islands of Twillingate. They were experiencing many difficulties getting from island to island, especially during the spring and fall, when they had ice floes as well as tides to contend with. John saw that a bridge was necessary and instigated a petition to be sent to the governor requesting this necessity. The petition, drawn up by Magistrate Peyton and presented to the governor, was instrumental in obtaining a grant for the construction of the bridge.

To the Honourable House of Assembly of Newfoundland in sessions convened: (circa 1844) The Petition of the undersigned, inhabitants of Twillingate, herewith,

That the population of Twillingate is about two thousand, nearly equally divided between the North and South sides of the

Magistrate John Peyton's home at Twillingate

harbour which varies from a mile to three quarters of a mile in width.

That at the southwest end or head of the harbour there is a Run or Tickle so called, about two hundred yards wide and which forms a connecting link between the said harbour and the Western Bight in Green Bay communicating with Exploits and other parts of the bay.

That your petitioners have long suffered great loss and inconvenience in consequence of not having a bridge across the above mentioned Tickle, to enable them to transact their various matters of business without the unavoidable use of boats to which they are now at all times obliged to resort whenever it becomes necessary for them pass from one side of the harbour to the other.

That is every season of the year, this inconvenience is felt by the inhabitants generally and also by strangers and visitors as one of magnitude, and especially is this evil apparent during the winter and spring months when the floating ice in the harbour for weeks together completely stops all communication between the people, except at great risk and hazard of life.

That your petitioners are of the opinion that the sum of three hundred pounds added to their own labour, would be sufficient to build the said bridge.

They therefore, pray that your Honourable House will take the matter into consideration and grant for such object any sum which to your Honourable House may seem meet.

And your petitioners shall ever pray.

The letter in reply to this request was sent by James Crowdy, the Governor's secretary, on May 8, 1844, in which the Governor appointed John Peyton, John Slade, Abraham Pearce and Samuel Prowse as commissioners for the proposed project. The letter reads as follows:

ST. JOHN'S, MAY 9, 1844

Gentlemen,
The Governor having been pleased to appoint you Commissioners for carrying into effect the following grant of

the Legislature, £250 to be appropriated in deepening the Tickle at Twillingate and in erecting a bridge across "the same provided that an equal sum be contributed by inhabitants of Twillingate for the purpose aforesaid."

I am directed by his Excellency to acquaint you that he will issue a warrant in your favour for £100 and that when he is satisfied that £200 have been expended on the work in question that is, the £100 paid by the Colony and £100 by the people of Twillingate, he will issue a second warrant in your favour for a similar amount to be expended with another sum of equal amount provided by the people.

> I have the honour to be, Gentlemen,
> Your most obedient servant.
> Signed: James Crowdy.

John Slade, one of the appointed Commissioners, took it upon himself while in St. John's to engage an engineer and buy the necessary tools needed for the job. The letter he wrote to John Peyton and the other commissioners reads:

Gentlemen,
I have the pleasure of forwarding you by Mr. Knight your appointments as a Board of Commissioners for superintending the erection of a bridge across the Tickle at Twillingate.

Knowing gentlemen, that some engineer would be necessary for superintending the work, both as regards the erection of the bridge as well as excavating the Tickle, I took upon myself to engage with Mr. Thomas Wells, an engineer from Nova Scotia for ten shillings per diem and to find himself, an act of which I trust you will approve.

I advanced the said Mr. Wells the sum of five pounds earning, receipt of which you will find enclosed...

The House of Messers. John Slade and Company has paid sum of £2. 17.9 for tools that he would have found it difficult to have obtained at Twillingate, the account to which you will find enclosed...

I also beg leave to forward to you Mr. Wells' agreement with me, which I trust will meet with your approbation...

Wishing you success in carrying out the wishes of the General Assembly.

I am, Gentlemen.
Yours most respectfully,
John Slade.

William F. Lee and Thomas Mahaney were hired as carpenters and Thomas Coyle was hired to do the dredging. The work was begun on Monday, June 17, 1844. A month later the dredging was completed and the groundwork of the abutments was set in place. As the work progressed the engineer Wells was warned of his intemperate behaviour in a letter form Magistrate Peyton.

JULY 5, 1844

To: Mr. Thomas Wells

Sir,
Having observed with much regret that you have not conducted yourself with that sobriety and attention which we had a right to expect from you and in many instances you have been in a state so as not to be enabled when to give satisfactory replies to questions which have been put to you relative to the work under your superintendence.

We have to intimate to you that unless you are more attentive and sober in future, we shall be under the disagreeable necessity of dispensing with your services in future.

We are, Sir, your obedient servants,
(signed) John Peyton
Samuel Prowse
Abraham Pearce, Commissioners.

A short time later Mr. Wells was dismissed and the work completed by the crew already engaged.

John worked daily out of the courthouse building at Twillingate. It was a two-storey building with a three-storey tower. The first floor contained living quarters for the constable and jailer, and two cells for the prisoners. The top floor was a large room in which there was an elevated platform where the judge sat, a large round table surrounded by chairs for the magistrate, sheriff, clerk and any barristers that might be present. On either side of the room were two long benches, one reserved for the grand jury when in session and the other for the common jury. Around the late 1830s, if members of the latter wished to consult one another in order to bring in a verdict, they were led out of doors by the constable and assembled on a rock close by, where they were "locked up"—in imagination—till they all agreed.[146]

At that time Twillingate's first policeman was Constable James Rice, a native of Collompton, Devonshire, who had come to Newfoundland in 1806. During the latter part of John's

North side of Twillingate

tenure as magistrate, the Twillingate policeman was Constable McKay.

When John and Eleanor moved to Twillingate in 1836 their family had increased to six. Three more children were later added to their family. John took great pride in his oldest

First bridge connecting the two islands of Twillingate, 1844 (note courthouse in background)

son John (John Henry), who bore his name. John Henry was twelve when he moved from Exploits Island to Twillingate. This was the young lad who during the first few years of his life had been cared for by Shanawdithit. He had already been introduced to river and sea travel at a very early age, for his father often took him along on his excursions by boat and schooner.

In 1837, at age thirteen, John Henry was sent to England to be educated at Christchurch School, his father's old school.

While there he was under the care of his grandmother and uncle James, both living at Wimborne. He showed exceptional intelligence and artistic ability and did well with his studies. The calligraphic illustrations depicted in the book are taken from John Henry's workbook of 1837.

For the next three years (1837–1840) John Henry crossed the Atlantic each spring and fall by schooner, to and from school in England. His passages were arranged with sea captains, generally friends of his father. The following letter received in 1838 from John's mother in England mentions John Henry.

WIMBORNE, SEPT. 17, 1838

My Dear Son,
I received your letter and was happy to find that you and family were in good health and have to inform you and Mrs. Peyton that your son is in good health at brothers. If you can make it convenient shall be obliged to you to send me some berries also a little wet fish [uncured] and some dry for the winter as it will be very acceptable. Hope Mrs. Peyton will like her cloak and bonnet. I have put in the box a green veil of mine for her. I have to beg her acceptance of it as it will match the bonnet. Don't forget to give my kind love to all the children also her. Write me the first opportunity. So conclude with my kind love to you from your affectionate mother.

(signed) Anne Peyton

P.S. You seemed to have in your mind that you should come to see me which would be great pleasure for us to meet. Give my respects to Capt. Rogers. Tell us if James Pike is living.

In 1839 Geologist J.B. Jukes was sent to Newfoundland from England to make a geological survey of the structure of the island. On his visits around the island he spent a month at Twillingate, where he accepted the hospitality of John Slade. At that time Jukes said that Slade "and Mr. Peyton were determined to accompany me on an excursion to the River Exploits."[147]

Slade and Jukes and their two servants journeyed to Exploits in Slade's yacht, while John and his son John Henry, home on his summer vacation, and the two servants left Twillingate by sailing skiff. The excursion started off early in September with the intention of returning in time for the annual court circuit and travelling judge's sessions at Twillingate. It was later learned that the judge arrived earlier than expected, and he was quoted as saying, "he had a great mind to run on and join us in our excursion up the river."[148]

The party had hopes of reaching Red Indian Lake, but the laborious journey, difficulty walking along the riverbanks and the tiring portages around the rapids, rocks and shoals in small flats, called for courage and quick decisions.

John, with Slade and the trapper Blake, managed one "flat" while John Henry, Jukes and Simon (Jukes's manservant) managed the second, John Henry as polesman, Jukes at the scull and Simon amidships.

The skill of those in the second flat were so good as to bring a remark for the old furrier Blake, "as if they had been used to the brook for twenty years."[149]

When they arrived at Twillingate it was found the brigs making their final fall departure for England had already left. Jukes, in order to arrange a passage home to England, would have to travel to St. John's. John also needed to secure a passage for his son John Henry to return to school. They left for St. John's on the schooner *Content*, which also carried a full load of dry salt cod for market. After a long and uncomfortable voyage they arrived at St. John's two weeks later, just in time to witness the arrival of the steamship *Spitfire*, the first of its kind ever to visit Newfoundland. The sailing skippers approaching the harbour when she arrived were "so astonished as she approached, that they had scarcely the presence of mind to get out of her way, and she had very nearly run them down."[150]

Jukes then took passage aboard the steamship *Spitfire* for England. John Henry also returned to England for his third year at Christchurch School. In April of the following spring, in a letter home he wrote:

My dear Parents,
I suppose you will feel a little disappointed in not seeing me by the first vessel instead of a letter from me. We were not aware that Capt. Quinton was going to sail so soon. He called on us Good Friday with Capt. Harvey and informed us that he should be off on Thursday. It will not be convenient for me to leave so soon, but I expect to embrace the next opportunity that offers, which I suppose will be in a short time. I believe Uncle James is writing to you, and no doubt he will inform you of the accident my poor Grandmother met with some time ago; this has occasioned me some loss of time at school, but I am happy to say she is much better. I have been doing something at navigation. I understand Logarithms tolerably well, and am nearly through plain Trigonometry. I hope you are both quite well, and all my brothers and sisters. I am very well myself. The weather has of late been very fine indeed.

> With kind love to all my friends.
> I remain, My dear parents,
> Your dutiful son,
> John H. Peyton

As John Henry prepared for his passage home he wrote
again:

WIMBORNE, MAY 8, 1840

My dear Parents,
I am very sorry to think that you will be again disappointed in finding that I am not to come with the *Montague*. I felt some reluctance
to trust myself in her; however, I think I should have ventured had
not Uncle been so unwilling. I do not much like the prospect of
waiting so long for Capt. Hutchins, as I hear he is not likely to sail
till July, and that he will probably take Hamburgh [sic] in his way. This
will considerably lengthen the passage, but it is some relief to my
anxiety to know that it will be in the summer season, and that I may
have the opportunity of seeing Hamburgh, which would be very
gratifying to me. The season in this country has of late been exceed-
ingly fine. I believe we had no rain during the month of April, but we
have had some beautiful showers yesterday and today and the
prospect is at present very cheering. I hope to hear from you soon.
Grandmother is better, as I suppose Uncle will inform you. I am
quite well, and hope all my dear friends at home are the same. With
kindest love to them all, I remain, My dear Parents,

Your dutiful and affectionate son,
John H. Peyton

This is believed to have been the last letter written to his
"dear parents" and the last communications that Eleanor and
John were to have from their young son, for on his way home
the ship was lost and he was assumed to have drowned.

This was a devastating blow to John and Eleanor. John's
hopes had rested in his son. The family name John was no
longer. John's plans of having his younger sons Thomas, Elias
and James educated in England were destroyed. Thomas, the
second son (who later became the grandfather of the author's
husband), was slated to study for the ministry.

Despite his grief at the loss of his oldest son, John was happy to see his three remaining sons later marry and settle in homes close to his own home. Thomas married Ann Pearce, Elias married Deborah Rideout and James married Ann Britt. All of these young women were from Twillingate. John's oldest daughter Ann (who had been cared for by Shanawdithit) married Dr. William Stirling Jr., a newcomer to Twillingate. They were to become the parents of Newfoundland's famous opera singer Georgina (Twillingate) Stirling (stage name Marie Toulinguet). Susan Peyton, the second daughter, married Albert Stirling (Dr. Stirling's brother) in 1862 and moved to English Harbour West, where she died in 1866 in childbirth. Both of John Peyton's younger daughters, Eleanor, aged twenty-one, and Georgina, aged ten, died during the month of March 1864 of diphtheria or smallpox.

Around 1870, at the age of seventy-nine years, John severed his final family ties with England, which he fondly referred to as "the land of my birth." In 1869 he had been requested to sell the property he still owned at Christchurch. A letter he received reads:

PUREWELL,
CHRISTCHURCH, ENG.
MARCH 19, 1869

To: Mr. Peyton, Esq.
Magistrate, Twillingate

Sir,
Having been informed that you are the owner of a piece of land with the remains of two cottages thereon (of which there is a great deal of dispute between parties as to possession and even law) a Mr. Frier* of Wimborne formerly took the rent but have [sic]

declined to take it this last fifteen years and now I think Sir George Tapps wants to lay hands on it, he being Lord of the Manor.

This piece of land is situated at a place called Purewell and I am told by an old inhabitant that it is freehold property and it belongs to you.

If the owner [ship] belongs to you and you feel disposed to sell I should like to know the price of the same.

The party that used to rent it is dead and now two other parties are continually wrangling about it.

Awaiting your reply, I remain

Yours truly,

(signed) George Pope.

John's reply to this letter is not recorded, but he apparently sold the property.

John suffered terribly in his last few remaining years from rheumatism. In his diary he entered:

MARCH 2, 1878:
Very fine but very cold. Suffering severely with rheumatic in left shoulder, almost paralysed [sic].

MARCH 3, 1878:
Sunday, fine and mild. Dr. Stirling and Mr. Owen called. Mrs. Stirling [daughter Ann] spent the afternoon. Arm and leg very stiff and painful.

MARCH 4, 1878:
Left shoulder very uneasy.

John's son Elias named his son John Henry II and in his teen years became his grandfather's close companion and helper. John, in his

John Peyton in later years

declining years, doted on this grandson and a close bond developed between grandfather and grandson. The aging John may have been reminded of his own son John Henry I. John's diary:

APRIL 1, 1878:
Most disagreeable day. Attended Quarter Sessions [Supreme Court on circuit], very full attendance. R.P. Rice forman.... Heavy glitter, trees loaded with ice, travelling bad.

APRIL 7, 1878:
Gloomy, stiff breeze and drizzling rain. 9 p.m. John Henry [grandson] dangerously attacked with ulceration sore throat [diptherial].

APRIL 8, 1878:
My poor little helpmate John Henry dying. This is a severe blow to me in my fast approaching fate, I may say. My mainstay and support for a few of my remaining miserable hours.... My poor dear boy died at 11 a.m. in peace and content without a struggle, retaining his senses to the last moment showing every symptom of thanks for kind treatment, the administration of his comforts.

APRIL 12, 1878:
Rev. Temple called. Made arrangements for interment.

APRIL 14, 1878: SUNDAY - 12 NOON.
Went and looking last sight of poor little dear companion, never to be forgotten.

Although fate had struck so many blows throughout John's lifetime, his spirit remained strong, and while suffering physical pain, he kept up his determination to carry on.

Owing to the fact that no other magistrate had been appointed to fill his post, he carried on his daily duties, assisted by his son Thomas, into his eighty-seventh year.

During John's long tenure in office as magistrate he made regular twice-yearly visits to Fogo Island, with occasional visits in between as his services were required. A Mr. Fitzgerald was later appointed magistrate for the Fogo district.

Altogether John Peyton served both governments, Imperial and Colonial, as boy and man, for sixty-four years. Although about six months before his death a pension was granted for those giving lengthy service, he never took advantage of this benefit.

In John's final years friends and associates often called to visit him. In 1878 he was visited by John Day. He wrote in his diary on March 1: "Weather fine but cold. John Day arrived from Rocky Bay [now Carmanville]." John Day was a former servant and fur trapper with Miller and Peyton Sr. and one of the crew of the Peyton expedition during the capture of Mary March. No doubt both men had much to reminisce about concerning that expedition of March 1819, fifty-nine years before.

John heard of the sighting of the old Slade vessel *John and Thomas* that had originally brought him to Newfoundland in 1812. Jack Wheeler of Twillingate, returning from Battle Harbour, Labrador, brought the news that he had seen the old sailing ship there. The brig had been completely renovated and refitted above the waterline but "below she was as solid as ever."

John died on July 25, 1879. His body was conveyed by boat to Exploits Burnt Island, in the Bay of Exploits, the bay that had become so dear to him. He was buried in the same grave as his father, one coffin resting upon the other, as was his wish.

The one horizontal slab of granite, four inches thick, marks the resting place of both father and son.

> Died- At Back Harbour, Twillingate, on the 25th July, John Peyton, Esq., a native of Christchurch, Hants, England, aged 87 years, 67 of which he spent in Newfoundland.
> For a period of 65 years he held H.M. Commission of the Peace, and for 43 years filled the responsible office of Stipendairy Magistrate for the District of Twillingate and Fogo. Deceased enjoyed the esteem of all his acquaintances, by whom his death is sincerely regretted.

The abandoned graveyard at Exploits Island. The horizontal granite slab marks the grave of both "Father and Son." (Photo: Brian Bursey)

Shortly before he died, John gave his son Thomas £5 to settle a debt he owed. It cannot be said he died in penury, for he owned property and had obtained a good living from his land. But when his son Thomas settled up his affairs after his death and paid what was legally due, he had to pay £30 out of his own pocket to complete the transaction. Thomas noted, "I may

[sic] have sold some of the movable property...but refrained from doing so, considering it was my duty to act by him as I knew he would have done by myself."

Later the Peyton rights and properties on the Exploits River were sold and were "in part purchased by Alfred Beaton, an old servant of John, from the executors of the late C.F. Bennett, who held mortgage on the property."[151]

This ended an era of entrepreneuring on the Exploits River by the Peyton pioneers. So the river lords were no more, but their lives had shaped the lives of many, as well as those who came after them.

The island of Exploits was vacated during the resettlement years of 1950s and '60s and left deserted for many years. The small graveyard looks unkempt and forgotten. The fences have fallen, the grass is overgrown. The tall grasses wave in

Ferry John Peyton *on the Twillingate to New World Island run in the 1960s.*

this winds as a ceaseless "ripple of tide" over the many forgotten pioneer graves. The sea alone keeps vigil.

To commemorate John Peyton's lengthy service of forty-three years as Twillingate's first magistrate, the car ferry (capable of carrying eighteen cars) linking Twillingate and New World Island in the 1960s, was named the *John Peyton*. At Back Harbour a small road is named Peyton Road. This road was formerly John's carriage road from the main road to his homestead.

Courthouse, Twillingate

Epilogue

John's son Thomas, who had worked closely with him, was to carry on in his father's tradition. Thomas's experience, coupled with endurance and fortitude, caused him to follow in his father's footsteps.

As a young man Thomas spent fourteen summers on the Exploits River salmon stations, supervising the operations of his father. He had later became a fishery warden for the rivers of Notre Dame Bay and was deeply concerned with salmon stock conservation, and saw to it that the "rack work" was removed from the rivers at set times. In his reports he was critical of the sawmills springing up in the Exploits valley, disposing of their sawdust by dumping it into the breeding brooks and rivers, smothering the spawning grounds.

He became a Member of the House of Assembly for Newfoundland, 1889–1893. During that time he took an active part in the conservation of lobsters in Notre Dame Bay. By 1890 the stocks were so depleted that only very small lobsters were being caught. He travelled around the bay for the government, placing floating incubators of lobster roe from the hatchery at Dildo, Trinity Bay, in various locations.

Before the completion of the Newfoundland railway Thomas travelled on foot and by dog team from Twillingate to Whitbourne (the railway terminus) in his determination to attend sessions of the House. When the railway was further completed as far as Port Blandford, he travelled on foot and dog team to Clode Sound, making the remaining passage by train.

Thomas was also made a Justice of the Peace, and for a short time was a magistrate at Pilley's Island. As a Deputy Land Surveyor he often worked with the well-known geologists Alexander Murray and James P. Howley.

Thomas Peyton in his later years (MHA for Newfoundland 1889-1893)

In an assessment of the Peyton pioneers, one is reminded of Winston Churchill's words: "The only guide to a man is his conscience; the only shield to his memory is the rectitude and sincerity of his actions."

ENDNOTES

1. Jukes, J.B., *Excursions in and about Newfoundland*, William Clowse and Sons, London, 1842.

2. Howley, James P., *The Beothuks or Red Indians*, Cambridge University Press, Cambridge, England, 1915.

3. *Ibid.* p. 3.

4. *Ibid.* p. 8.

5. *Ibid.* p. 7.

6. Hunt, Robert M., *The Life of Sir Hugh Palliser*, Chapman Hall, London, 1844.

7. Howley, *op. cit.* p. 35.

8. Howley, *op. cit.* p. 49.

9. Peyton, Thomas, *Journal*, documents and letters. (Thomas Peyton, Justice of the Peace, Deputy and Land Surveyor, Fishery Warden, Magistrate, M.H.A. 1889-1893).

10. Howley, *op. cit.* p. 26.

11. Howley, *op. cit.* p. 26.

12. Originally named Lieutenant's Lake, then Lake Bathurst; now Red Indian Lake.

13. Prowse, D.W., *A History of Newfoundland*, Macmillan and Company, London, New York, 1895, p. 385.

14. Settlers carrying on a business (e.g. fishing or trapping) for themselves, with servants of their own, but supplied by a merchant in trade for the produce of their work.

15. Peyton, T., *op. cit.*

16. *Ibid.*

17. *Ibid.*

18. *Ibid.*

19. *Ibid.*

20. *Ibid.*

21. Wilson, Reverend William, *Newfoundland and its Missionaries*, Cambridge, Massachusetts, 1866.

22. Peyton, *op. cit.*

23. *Ibid.*

24. *Ibid.*

25. Pulling, Captain, *Pulling Report*, Newfoundland Room, Memorial University, St. John's, Nfld., Canada.

26. *Ibid.*

27. Peyton, T., *op. cit.*

28. Prowse, *op. cit.*, p. 280.

29. Peyton, T., *op. cit.*

30. *Ibid.*

31. *Ibid.*

32. *Ibid.*

33. Fishery Report 1872. (Thomas Peyton, Fishery Warden).

34. Peyton, T., *op. cit.*

35. *Ibid.*

36. Greek mythology.

37. Peyton, T., *op. cit.*

38. Howley, *op. cit.* p. 48.

39. Felled trees to form a fence, diverting the caribou herds to the river for easier targets.

40. Peyton, Colonel John Lewis, *The Adventures of my Grandfather*, John Wilson, Publisher, London, 1867.

41. *New England Historical and Genealogical Register*, Vol. 35, Washington, D.C., 1881.

42. Peyton, T., *op. cit.*

43. Peyton Papers (documents).

44. Specified kind of merchandise; in this case salmon and furs.

45. In nautical usage; canvas sails.

46. A fisherman's term, signifying the whole of the implements used; boats, nets, hooks and lines, etc.

47. Whiting, C.J., *History of the Lodge of Hengist #195*, W. Mate and Sons, Bournemouth; G. Kenning, London, 1897.

48. Jukes, *op. cit.*

49. Howley, *op. cit.*, p. 56.

50. Pulling, *op. cit.*

51. English youths, in the first few years of their servitude as appren-

tices, to guard river claims.

52. Peyton, T., *op. cit.*

53. *Ibid.*

54. Howley, *op. cit.*, p. 106.

55. *Ibid.* p. 106.

56. *Ibid.* p. 91.

57. *Ibid.* p. 92.

58. *Ibid.* p. 108.

59. *Ibid.* p. 93.

60. *Ibid.* p. 93.

61. *Ibid.* p. 106.

62. *Ibid.* p. 72.

63. *Ibid.* p. 80.

64. *Ibid.* p. 106.

65. *Ibid.* p. 281.

66. *Ibid.* p. 281.

67. *Ibid.* p. 273.

68. Ibid. p. 281.

69. Peyton documents.

70. Howley, *op. cit.* p. 323.

71. *Ibid.* p. 344.

72. *Ibid.* p. 94.

73. *Ibid.* p. 108.

74. *Ibid.* p. 105.

75. *Ibid.* p. 107.

76. *Ibid.* p. 120.

77. *Ibid.* p. 110.

78. *Ibid.* p. 114.

79. *Ibid.* p. 120.

80. *Ibid.* p. 120.

81. *Ibid.* p. 115.

82. *Ibid.* p. 115.

83. Peyton papers.

84. Howley, *op. cit.* p. 117

85. Peyton documents.

86. Howley, *op. cit.* p. 116.

87. *Ibid.* p. 121.

88. *Ibid.* p. 121.

89. *Ibid.* p. 121.

90. *Ibid.* p. 121.

91. Peyton, T., *op. cit.*

92. Howley, *op. cit.* p. 125.

93. *Ibid.* p. 121.

94. Jukes, *op. cit.* p. 150

95. Peyton, T., *op. cit.*

96. *Ibid.*

97. Supplies of provisions and utensils.

98. Copper pot in possession of Edgar Baird, Gander, a great-grandson of John Peyton, Jr.

99. Howley, *op. cit.* p. 127.

100. Murray, Alexander, *Geological Survey of Newfoundland,* Edward Stanford, London, 1881.

101. *Ibid.* p. 357.

102. Peyton, T., *op. cit.*

103. Inglis, Bishop John, *Report of the Society of the Propagation of the Gospel in Foreign Parts.* 1827.

104. The fishing area designated by treaty to the French.

105. Believed to be a brother-in-law of John Peyton, Jr.

106. Poem by Ernest Peyton, great-grandson of John Peyton, Jr.

107. Howley, *op. cit.* p. 175, 180 and 181.

108. *Ibid.* p. 172.

109. *Ibid.* p. 173.

110. *Ibid.* p. 300.

111. *Ibid.* p. 182.

112. *Ibid.* p. 182.

113. *Ibid.* p. 176.

114. *Ibid.* p. 297.

115. Inglis, *op. cit.* p. 87.

116. In nautical usage, to haul by a line fastened to a dock, generally in berthing sailing ships when winds are unfavourable.

117. Inglis, *op. cit.*

118. *Ibid.* p. 84.

119. John Peyton's diary.

120. Inglis, *op. cit.* p.87.

121. *Ibid.* p. 87.

122. *Ibid.* p. 84.

123. Howley, *op. cit.* p. 282.

124. Inglis, *op. cit.* p. 87.

125. Howley, *op. cit.* p. 205.

126. *Evening Telegram,* May 26, 1956.

127. Howley, *op. cit.* p. 186.

128. *Ibid.* p. 186.

129. *Evening Telegram,* May 26, 1956.

130. Howley, *op. cit.* p. 195.

131. Ibid. p. 322.

132. Poem by Ernest Peyton.

133. *Ibid.*

134.Howley, *op. cit.* p. 201.

135. *Ibid.* p. 202.

136. *Evening Telegram*, May 26, 1956.

137. Fay, C.R., *Life and Labour in Newfoundland*, University of Toronto Press, Toronto, 1956, p. 101.

138. Howley, *op. cit.* p. 203.

139. *Ibid.* p. 202.

140. *Ibid.* p. 208.

141. *Ibid.* p. 210.

142. *Evening Telegram*, May 26, 1956.

143. *Ibid.*

144. Peyton, T., *op. cit.*

145. Ibid.

146. Jukes, *op. cit.* p. 153.

147. *Ibid.* p. 119, Vol. 11.

148. *Ibid.* p. 151.

149. *Ibid.* p. 148.

150. Ibid. p. 173.

151. Peyton, T., *op. cit.*

BIBLIOGRAPHY

Bruton, F.A. *Narrative of a Journey Across the Island of Newfoundland* (W.E. Cormack), Longmans, Green and Company, London, New York, Toronto.

Buchan, Captain David *Journal 1810-1811.*

Fay, C.R. *Life and Labour in Newfoundland,* University of Toronto Press, Toronto, 1956.

Head, C. Grant. *Eighteenth Century Newfoundland,* McClelland and Stewart, Toronto, 1976.

Horwood, Joan. *William Epps Cormack,* Bishop Printing Ltd., St. John's.

Howley, James P. *The Beothuks or Red Indians,* Cambridge University Press, Cambridge, England, 1915.

Hunt, Robert M. *The Life of Sir Hugh Palliser,* Chapman Hill, London, 1844.

Inglis, Bishop John *Report of the Society for the Propagation of the Gospel in Foreign Parts.* 1827.

Jukes, J.B. *Excursions in and about Newfoundland,* W. Clowse and Sons, London, 1842.

"Liverpool Manuscript," Newfoundland Rooms, Memorial University, St. John's.

Mansions and Merchants of Poole and Dorset. Poole Historical Trust, Vol. 1, 1976.

Murray, Alexander. *Geological Survey of Newfoundland*, Edward Stanford, London, 1881.

Peyton, Colonel John Lewis. *The Adventures of my Grandfather*, John Wilson, London, 1867.

Prowse, D.W. *A History of Newfoundland*, Macmillan and Company, London, New York 1895.

Pulling, Captain G.C. *"Pulling Report,"* Newfoundland Room, Memorial University, St. John's.

Rowe, F.W. *Extinction: The Beothuk Indians of Newfoundland*, McGraw Hill Ryerson, Toronto, 1977.

Smith, Reverend Canon Walter B. "Notes of Church and Secular History of Notre Dame Bay."

Townsend, C.W. *Captain Cartwright and his Labrador Journal*, Colonial Press, Boston.

Toque, Reverend Phillip. *Newfoundland as it was, and as it is in 1877*, John B. Magurn, Toronto, 1878.

Wilson, Reverend William. *Newfoundland and its Missionaries*, Cambridge, Massachusetts, 1866.

Whiting, C.J. *History of the Lodge of Hengist #195*, W. Mate and Sons, Bournemouth; George Kenning, London, 1897.

Newspapers: *The Newfoundlander, The Evening Telegram, Royal Gazette*. Private collection of papers, letter and photographs of Ernest A. Peyton. Private collection of paper and letters of Edgar A. Baird.

Appendix I

THE YOUNGER JOHN'S RECIPES
OF THE EARLY 1800s

To make Currant Wine

Take 8 quarts of juice of currants, 12 quarts of water, 18 lbs. of moist sugar; mix it in a tub and let it stand 24 hours. Then put it into a barrel and then put a quart of brandy into it and stop it up close after a few days.

To make Gooseberry Wine

To every pound of gooseberries, well bruised, put in one quart of water. Let it stand three days, stirring every day. Then strain the juice and to every gallon put three pounds of lump sugar. Put it into a cask and to every five gallons put one quart of brandy. Let it stand six months and then bottle it. The gooseberries should be full grown and should be used when they are in proper state for bottling. You must not bury up [close up] the barrel until the wine has done singing.

Ginger Beer

1 ½ oz. of Ginger well bruised, 1 oz. of Cream of Tartar and 1 lb. loaf sugar. Put these ingredients into an earthen vessel and pour upon them a gallon of boiling water. When cold add a tablespoonful of yeast and let the whole stand til the next morning. Then skim it, bottle it and keep it three days in a cool place before you use it. Be sure to use good corks and clean them with brine or wire.

To make Parsnip Wine

Take 4 gallons of parsnips sliced thin (heaped measure), boil them in 10 gallons of water till quite soft, then squeeze them well and add to every gallon of liquor, 3 lbs. of moist sugar. Let it boil 3/4 of an hour. When nearly cold put in a tablespoon of yeast and let it stand for a week, stirring it well every day and when the fermentation ceases bring it close. The proper time for making it is March.

To make Ginger Wine

Take four gallons of spring water and 7 lbs. of Lisbon sugar, boil them for a 1/4 of an hour and keep skimming it well. When the liquor is cold, squeeze in the juice of two lemons, boil the peels with 2 ozs. of Ginger in 3 pints of water and for one hour. When this is cold put it all together into a barrel with two spoonfuls of yeast, 1/4 oz. of isinglass beat very thin, and 2 lbs. of jar raisins. Close it up and let it stand seven weeks, then bottle it. The best season to make it is in the spring.

Raspberry or Currant Wine

To every three pints of fruit (cleaned carefully from mouldy or bad) put one quart of water, bruise the former. In 24 hours strain the liquor and put to every quart a pound of sugar, of good middling quality of Lisbon. If for white currants, use lump sugar. It is best to put the fruit in a large pan and when in 3 or 4 days the scum rises, take that off before the liquor is put into the barrel.

Lemon Wine

Strip the rind of 2 dozen lemons, pared very thin, in a gallon of spirits for 24 hours. Then squeeze the juice on 2 lbs. of common lump sugar and 5 quarts water. Mix all ingredients together and pour on them three pints of boiling milk. Let stand 24 hours, then strain it through a thick blanketing jelly bag till quite clear. Half rum and half brandy is considered better than brandy.

To make Cheese

Warm the milk as warm as it comes from the cow in the summer season, and in the winter season it must be heated hotter, and put a large spoonful of rennet to every 4 gallons of milk. When the milk is turned into curds stir it up well and let it pitch. Then take away the whey and break the curds up well and strain them dry of the whey. Salt them well and break them up small. Take a cheese cloth and put it over the vat and put as much of the curds into it as it will hold; turn the ends of the cloth over it and tuck it into the vat, put it in a press to press the whey out. Take it out of the vat and turn it over and let it remain in the press one day. Then take it out and put some salt upon it for 2 days. Afterwards turn it every day till it is dry; which if neglected will spoil the cheese.

To salt Beef, Pork, Mutton

Take four gallons of good water, to which add 1 ½ lbs. of molasses, two ounces saltpetre and six lbs. of common large salt. Put the whole in a clean kettle and let it boil, being careful to take off all the scum as it comes up; when no more arises, take the liquor off and let it stand till cold. Then having put the meat you want to preserve into a vessel you intend to keep it in, pour the liquor over the meat till it is quite covered, in which condition it must be kept. Beef salted in this manner has been taken out of the pickle after laying in it ten weeks, and found as good as if not salted more than three days and at the same time as tender as a chick.

To make Elder Wine

Add as many gallons of water as many gallons of Elderberries, boil 1/4 of an hour, then strain it well and add 3 lbs. sugar to a gallon or 3 ½ lbs. if it is to be kept long and 1/4 lb. all-spice, 1/4 lb. ginger and 1/4 lb. cloves to the proportion of 20 gallons of wine; the spices in a bag. Then boil it together about 3/4 of an hour, that you may properly skim it. Pour it into a tub till cold. Bake a slice of bread and dip it in yeast and put it into the tub to remain 2 or 3 days till you put it into a cask. N.B. The spices to be put loose into a cask with the wine.

To pot [earthenware crock] a Lobster

Half boil them, pick out meat, cut in small bits. Season with mace, white pepper, nutmeg and salt. Press close into a pot and cover with butter. Bake for ½ hour. Put the spawn in; when cold take the lobster out and put in into pots, with a little of the butter. Beat the other butter into a mortar with some of the spawn, then mix that coloured butter with as much as will be sufficient to cover the pots and strain it. Cayenne may be added if approved.

To jug [earthenware crock] a Hare

After skinning and cleaning, cut it up and season it with pepper and salt, allspice, grounded mace and a little nutmeg. Put it into a jar with an onion, a clove or two, a bunch of stout herbs, a piece of corned beef and the carcass bones over all. Tie the jar down with a bladder and leather, or strong paper and put it into a saucepan of water up to the neck but no higher. Keep the water boiling five hours. When it is to be served boil the gravy up with a piece of butter and flour, and if the meat gets cold, warm it in this, but not to boil.

Cutlets

Cut slices about 3/4 of an inch thick. Beat them with a rolling pin and wet them on both sides with egg. Dip them in a seasoning of breadcrumbs, parsley, thyme, marjoram, pepper, salt and nutmeg. Then put them into papers folded over and broil them. Have in a [gravy] boat melted butter with a little mushrooms.

To pickle Salmon

Cut the fish into proper pieces; do not take off the scales. Make a brine strong enough to bear an egg, in which boil the fish. It must be boiled in only just liquor enough to cover it. Do not over boil it. When the fish is boiled lay it slantingly to drain off all the liquor the salmon was boiled in, having first well skimmed it, and best vinegar. Let them rest for a day, then fill up again striking the sides of the kit [wooden tub made of staves and hoops] till it will receive no more, then head them down as close as possible. The above is given as the mode adopted for pickling salmon for the London market. [This recipe is signed Lady H., possibly Lady Hamilton.]

To pickle Salmon

Cut the salmon in pieces of 1½ to 2 lbs. Set it on the fire in a fish kettle with water sufficient to cover it and plenty of salt. As soon as it boils set it aside to simmer gently until done. Then remove it from the fire and let it remain in the liquor till cold. Then lay the pieces close together in a tub to pickle, sprinkling over it a small quantity of powdered saltpetre. Then put on top of the salmon liquor in which it was first boiled and add to it the same quantity of white wine vinegar, put it on the fire to skim and boil it 2 or 3 minutes; then take it off and when cold pour it over the salmon and tie it down and in three days turn in. In a week it is fit to use. [This recipe was also signed Lady H.].

Appendix II
OLD DOCUMENTS

Will of Harry Miller, 1775

157

List of provisions for the HM sloop Grasshopper

Handwritten marriage certificate of John Peyton and Eleanor Mananey, 1823

which is a small Rock: about four fathoms Water
on it.   Cromwells ledge lays from Little Fogo
Island distance about fifteen miles its dry
Shoal lays nearly N W. and breaks for half
a Mile in a moderate Sea
        Funk Island lays Ee. E from the
Round Head of Fogo. distance 10 Leagues.

For Frost Burnt

Goose grease smeared warm & the operation
often repeated never let the part be dry but
always covered with Grease

Virgin Rocks

Lat.t 46.26.23 N Long 50.56.35 ⅌ Cap.t Bishop H M B Manly
    46..35.   Long.50.51..   ⅌ Kemp.

Lat Cape Charles. 52..12 Long 55..51   Var. 35

La.t Phillips Brook Bay of Exploits
La L 49.14.10 N. Long .55..12.30 W
    Exploits Burnt Island _ 54..58..30 W.
        H M S Orestes - Cap.t Jones R.N July 1827.

July 2d 1827. H M S Orestes arrived of L W Isle with
        Bishop of Nova Scotia & Suit accompanied
    them up the Exploits. visited Bishops falls - River
                                                Exploits

A page from John's diary noting the visit of Bishop Inglis, 1827

MY SON,

hear the instruction of

THY FATHER,

and forsake not the law of

THY MOTHER.

...t dust is never done till it has raised in its consequences. Long after the stone has sunk to the bottom, never to rise again, the surface of the stream is troubled with the whirls of its plunge.

Polar Star —

Erect and adjust the Instrument
set the needle and arrow at 360°
bring down the Star and watch it
it carefully — after it attains its
altitude viz. a, as soon as it
appears to go East — clamp the
Instrument leaving it stand
untill morning — after deducting
-1.59" from the reading — put in
a stake and draw a pencil line
which will be a true meridian
line — as explained to me
by "James P. Howley Esqr
July 1886

Exploring River

Thomas Peyton

To locate the Polar Star.
Taken from the notebook of Thomas Peyton
as explained to him by James P. Howley, 1886.

164

To. Reduse square links
into. Acres. into Roods & perch.

Cut-off 5. figures. on right hand
side of product - and the five
those on the left will be Acres. and
the five remaining decimals of an
Acre, - Reduce these decimals into
Roods. by multipling by four, and
cut of 5. as. before. and multiply
the. last remaining decimals
by forty. cut off 5. again for perch
then you will have. the Area in
Acres. Rood and perces -
when the decimals. are less then 5
add. ciphers to the left hand side
when the remainder is less then
half a perch - it is rejected
when more it is called a perch
as. 0·02. is rough - 0·4. a perch -

Instructions on how to reduce square links

165

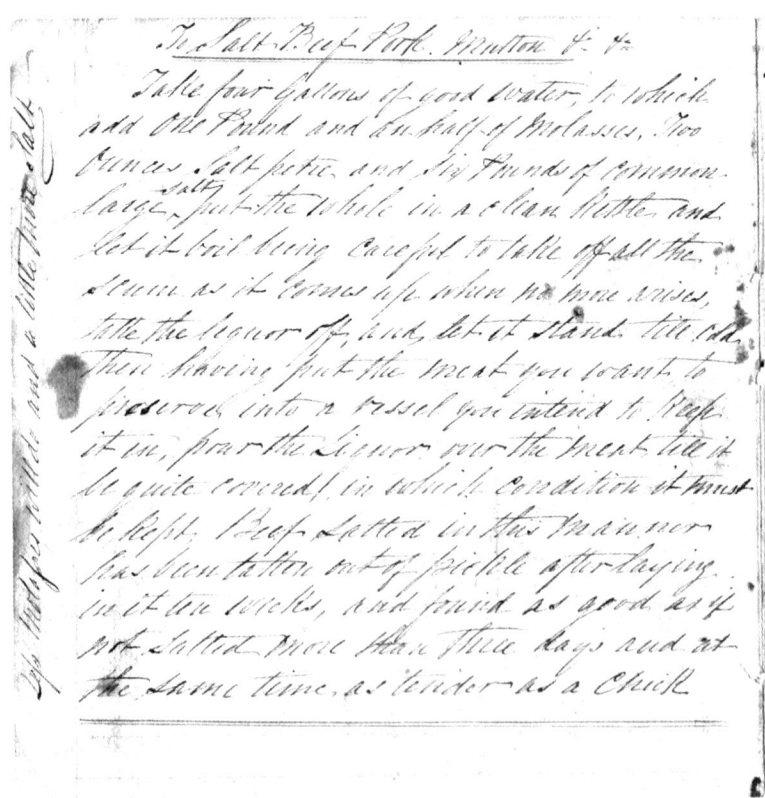

J. PEYTON

John Peyton's nameplate

Recipe for Salt Beef Pork Mutton

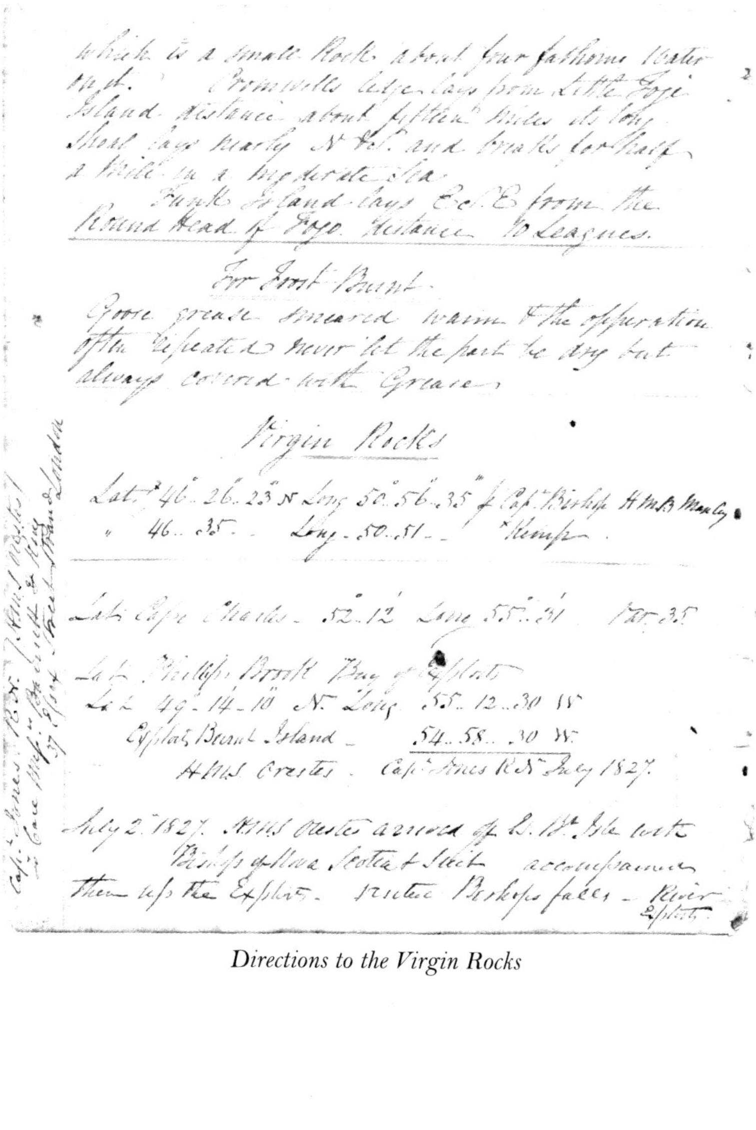
which is a small Rock about four fathoms water on it. Cromwells ledge lays from Little Fogo Island distance about fifteen miles its long shoal lays nearly N Wt. and breaks for half a mile in a moderate sea.

Funk Island lays E b N. E from the Round Head of Fogo distance 10 Leagues.

For Frost Burnt

Goose grease smeared warm & the opperation often repeated never let the part be dry but always covered with Grease.

Virgin Rocks

Latd 46°..26'..23" N Long 50°..56'..35" of Capt. Bishop HMS Manly
" 46..35.. Long..50..51.. " Kemp.

Lat. Cape Charles .. 52..12' Long 55..31 Var. 35

Lat. Phillips Brook Bay of Exploits
Lat 49°..14..10 N. Long 55..12..30 W
Exploits Burnt Island .. 54..58..30 W.
HMS Orestes .. Capt. Jones R.N. July 1827.

July 2nd 1827. HMS Orestes arrived off L. Bd. Isle with Bishop of Nova Scotia & suit accompanied them up the Exploits. visited Bishops falls .. River Exploits.

Capt. Jones R.N. HMS Orestes
Care Messrs Barrick & King
37 Great Tower St London

Directions to the Virgin Rocks

The following table will show to the nearest minute how much a clock should be faster or slower than a sun dial; such a table should be put upon every horizontal sun-dial.

Days of Month	Minutes	Days of Month	Minutes	Days of Month	Minutes	Days of Month	Minutes
Jan. 1	4	April 1	4	Aug. 9	5	Oct. 27	16
3	5	4	3	15	4	Nov. 15	15
5	6	7	2	20	3	20	14
7	7	11	1	24	2	24	13
9	8	15	0	28	1	27	12
12	9	*		31	0	30	11
15	10	19	1	*		Dec. 2	10
18	11	24	2	Sept. 3	1	5	9
21	12	30	3	6	2	7	8
25	13	May 13	4	9	3	9	7
31	14	29	3	12	4	11	6
Feb. 10	15	June 5	2	15	5	13	5
21	14	10	1	18	6	16	4
27	13	15	0	21	7	18	3
Mar. 4	12	*		24	8	20	2
8	11	20	1	27	9	22	1
12	10	25	2	30	10	24	0
15	9	29	3	Oct. 3	11	*	
19	8	July 5	4	6	12	26	1
22	7	11	5	10	13	28	2
25	6	28	6	14	14	30	3
28	5			19	15		

A chart showing the difference in accuracy between a clock and a sundial

An invoice of provisions and victualling for the schooner Susan *(Side 1)*

An invoice of provisions and victualling for the schooner Susan *(Side 2)*

Amy Louise (Anstey) Peyton is Newfoundland-born and educated at Twillingate and New York. She married in the United States in 1943. She has lived at Gander, Newfoundland, since 1946, where she settled with her husband, Ernest A. Peyton, ex-R.A.F. and one-time Councillor and Deputy Mayor of the town.

Amy and her husband became Gander's first florists and horticulturists. Since raising a family of five children, in her retirement she has turned her interest to music, creative crafts and writing. *River Lords: Father and Son* is her second book. Her first book, *Nightingale of the North*, published by Jesperson Press in 1984, tells the story of Newfoundland's opera prima donna Georgina Stirling, who gained international fame at the end of the nineteenth century.